HOW TO CREATE EVENTS TO REMEMBER

HOW TO CREATE EVENTS TO REMEMBER

Event Experts Share Their Success Secrets

LEE RICHTER
CERTIFIED MASTER COACH

HOW TO CREATE EVENTS TO REMEMBER: Event Experts Share Their Success Secrets
Copyright © 2018 Lee Richter

BMD Publishing
All Rights Reserved

ISBN # 978-1978447929

BMDPublishing@MarketDominationLLC.com
MarketDominationLLC.com

BMD Publishing CEO: Seth Greene
Editorial Management: Bruce Corris
Technical Editor & Layout: Kristin Watt

Cover Photo courtesy of FigTree Wedding Photography

Printed in the United States of America

DEDICATION

This book is dedicated to all the event planning professionals, who spend countless hours creating magical experiences and unforgettable memories. Every detail is important and I applaud you for sharing your passion and expertise.

To Gary, my loving husband who is patient with me as I help entrepreneurs around the world. I'm so grateful we met so early in life, and together, we continue to accomplish our dreams.

To Abbey, you are the daughter we adore. You have created an abundance of love and happiness in our family. You inspire me to be the best I can be. Thank you!

To my team, you are the support and inspiration making magic happen.

ACKNOWLEDGMENTS

As a little girl, I learned dreams could be achieved through hard work and perseverance. My parents guided me through those early years, navigating the business demands on a child model and keeping it fun and something I enjoyed. As a teen, statements like "LIVE YOUR DREAM" and "CREATE YOUR OWN HAPPINESS" resonated with me. My aspirations and dreams grew bolder and by college, I felt fearless. Entering the Merrill Lynch workforce in the '80's, required a brave young professional who would innovate and take risks based on a successful vision. Professional life taught me the most important life lesson: mentorship is the greatest path to GIVE and also GROW. I'm grateful for the life changing friends that have shared their gifts of time and knowledge to impact my life. Joe Polish, your Genius Network has been the most transformational friendship bonds of my adult life. These relationships are the energy source of innovation across all industries. You've taught me how "giving" leadership can create exponential growth and how it can align to our personal passions. Dan Sullivan, Strategic Coach has been the foundation of leadership and business skills. Your frameworks helped me grow my businesses in systematic and confident path. And, my friend Lisa Nichols, who's ability to motivate the masses is continuously inspiring me with Event Planners.

There's a special feeling in my heart when creating memorable experiences for others. These can be small deeds that occur that brightens a person day, sometimes this can be "paying it forward." The unique role Event Planners have is creating an extraordinary memory in the lives of others. Whether a wedding, 50th anniversary or a milestone birthday...people are in search of a planner who can create a vision and deliver an incredible experience. Often this is with the smallest direction or a budget a fraction of what's necessary, but somehow and someway, there's an Event Planner who creates the most memorable milestone in their lives. When you think about it, an Event Planner enters the clients lives briefly yet with the responsibility of a lifetime. Our industry is so extraordinary, delivering a gift so memorable, that guests will talk about it for years and the photos will bring back the magical feeling. Yet the planner who juggled a vast breadth of skills from business operations, marketing, finance and set the vision to create something unique in our lives, has moved on to creating the next miracle. That's what we do...we create!

Thank you every event planner who continues to create magical moments!

INTRODUCTION

Make it memorable. Make it magical. Make it exciting, enjoyable and time well spent.

We all know these are goals of an event planner. Whatever the event, whether it's small and intimate or large enough to fill a conference center, we want it to be successful. Whether it's a wedding that will create memories to last a lifetime, or a business meeting designed to improve business. We want it to be special. Our client wants it to be effective and memorable.

Whatever the event, the goals are often the same; Create something that does what it sets out to do and will be remembered for all the right reasons. And by the way, we want it to accomplish all that without leaving the event planner exhausted, stressed out, and wondering why on earth they're in this profession in the first place.

So how do you do that? How do you make it a great event without exhausting yourself in the process? How do you do it at a price that's good for your clients and for your business? How do you combine creativity, productivity, memorability and achieve profitability? And how do you have fun along the way? Because let's face it, this is not an easy gig or a high-paying one. We'd better enjoy ourselves when we go through all this effort.

One of the tools to create the best events is our knowledge. Knowing best practices. Knowing what works and what doesn't. Knowing what to do and what to avoid. Of course you get that knowledge through experience. But it doesn't just have to be your own experience for you to benefit.

At the Event Planners Club, one of our most important goals is to help our members get knowledge through the community. That's why we've created a place where members share their experiences and their knowledge with each other.

And that's why I decided to publish this book with interviews from some of the best event planners and other professions in the industry. Experts making memorable experiences who are willing to share their expertise with all of us are generous and we appreciate them very much.

Get ready to tap into this community. Get insights. Get case studies. Above all, increase your knowledge and contacts to help your business be more successful.

Cheers to creating events to remember!

TABLE OF CONTENTS

Live the life
you have
imagined.

CHAPTER 1
Meet Lee Richter

Our EPC community is very special! My joy is creating a place where we can grow our business and be inspired among friends and professionals sharing our passion for event planning.

Before you read about the amazing event planners we interviewed to get their insights and advice, I thought I would share a little by answering questions that people often ask me. How did I get my start in event planning? How did I develop my passion for creating an awesome experience? How did I become the CEO of an organization that helps thousands of event planners? And why did we create this book?

It's funny, I took a roundabout way to get here, and in many ways, I've come full circle. You see, I actually started in the advertising and event space when I was just six years old. I grew up by the Jersey shore in Neptune, New Jersey where I come from a typical middle class family. My dad was an engineer and my mom was a teacher who eventually became a nurse. And when I was the magical age of six, I started doing commercials.

Yes, I was a show-biz kid. I was in commercials for Clairol Shampoo, Oscar Mayer hot dogs, Wonder Bread and other national products. Remember the TV show *Dark Shadows*? I was in a commercial for Lipton Noodle Soup, which sponsored that show. Every time my mom watched *Dark Shadows*, my commercial came on and she was excited to see it. It was an interesting time in my life, however, I didn't realize how unique it was. At that time, I thought everyone lived like me. Later I realized, going to New York City and being on camera, having photography shoots, and doing interviews was quite a special experience. I'm grateful for that time in my life.

And during that time, there were always a lot of events to attend. Each time there was a commercial launch they would throw a party for the talent and for the crew. They catered our lively lunches and they catered our gourmet dinners. It was an interesting world that I was exposed to at such a young age. I will point out that it wasn't my choice. It was my mom who got my career started. She entered me into *Little Miss America* and I was discovered by an agent, Dick Miller. For the next six or seven years, I traveled to New Your City for interviews, auditions, photo shoots and production shoots. I became a member of the Screen Actors Guild and I received a SAG card at the age of seven. At times, it was very exciting. Sometimes it was exhausting. And most of the time, it was a lot of work. And one thing I noticed was that I just wanted to have more time with my friends. Like any kid, playing and being a kid was way more fun. I asked my mom if I could retire from the acting scene just before I turned 13. And I did.

Fast forward to when I graduated college. My first job was with Merrill Lynch. At one of the college job fairs, I interviewed with them. They said I was a good match for what they were looking for so I accepted a position. When I started working with Merrill Lynch, I noticed that the investment industry had interesting assignments that were similar to the advertising industry. A lot of the outreach and energy directed to connecting with the ideal customer is built around events and special occasions. We would have events where we would invite people and educate them how to invest their finances and we would celebrate birthdays, milestones and special occasions with our internal and external audiences.

When we hosted educational seminars, I discovered I really enjoyed it. So that was basically how I got into event planning, through marketing. Marketing is the umbrella and under it are creative business growth tactics. The goal is to connect with our ideal clients and to build relationships. One of the tactics used in marketing is event planning. Another tactic is public relations. Another is social media. I started seeing how each marketing effort is connected and I learned that I really like the entire process.

So how did this lead to the Event Planners Club? Long before the EPC came into existence, I was planning and hosting events during my finance career. Those years also gave me a strong financial background. I even went back to college and earned a degree in journalism and public relations because I realized how important that knowledge is in business and in life.

Now, at the EPC, I use all of those experiences and skills working with our members and helping them identify and accomplish their goals. I've spent a lot of time connecting with them. Those conversations are one of the reasons for this book. Many event planners have told me what they need most is help running their business. They need information, guidance, and mentorship to build a strategy and to better understand marketing. Many tell me they want to be connected to industry leaders and to other people in the community.

Connecting with global leaders is one of the things I really love about what I do. I'm curious all the time. When I meet people I'm always asking, "What's lighting you up right now?" I can't wait to get those answers and to learn more about people and what they're excited about. I mentioned earlier how much I love sharing people's stories. You can't share them if you don't know them. I love hearing their stories and what is important to them and then sharing it with others through media, social media and speaking events.

What makes a great event? People ask me this all the time. It's such a simple question but it's oh-so-complicated as well. There are many, many things that go into answering that question. But let's start here. I know it's a great event when I am sitting in the debrief meeting afterward and it feels good. It feels successful. It feels like I've accomplished something. If it's a wedding, the bride and groom are thrilled, the gifts are where they need to go, the food was wonderful, the music was great and the guests are happy. All those things go well and at the end I kick my feet up and think, "That was a great experience!" It was great for me as the provider of the event, for the people who came to the event and for the people who worked the event. It feels like an exceptional and successful experience.

A successful event is an experience that creates a good feeling for the people involved.

Event planners often take projects that are not a good choice. Whether it's because the business is needed or it could be lucrative or it could lead to something else. I've said yes to projects that I have regretted because of those reasons too. Fortunately, as I've advanced in my career, I get to choose my clients and who I spend time with. That's why I stick to easy and fun as criteria that is important to me. If it's not the ideal client for me, I find someone who's a better match for them. In the end, I always want them to be successful and to have a lovely event.

That's what event planning does when you're firing on all cylinders. It creates a feeling. The experience creates a feeling, and it's a feeling you want to experience again. It's that lightning in a bottle moment when a great event appears effortless. The key word there is "appears." It appears effortless but you know a lot of work goes into it.

Sometimes to get to unforgettable moments you have to get through many moments you can't wait to forget. Every event has challenges to overcome. It's inevitable. The key is to turn challenges into learning opportunities and to make sure to know what to avoid in the future. Some things that are important may not work sometimes, like when the timing is off or there is a technical failure. We once had a wedding cake fall to the ground. We had warned the family to keep the kids away from the cake. Obviously you can't get another wedding cake in five minutes, so we had to improvise with dozens of cupcakes from a local bakery. Because this type of thing has happened before, we now actually incorporate it into a plan "B" for the future. A big part of planning is doing your due diligence and homework. Know what choices you have in best-case scenarios and when you need to implement plan "B." Talking to people who have been there and learning from those who have walked that path before can shorten a learning curve dramatically.

As we've talked with our members of the Event Planners Club, the benefit of learning from others keeps coming up. They're now connected to thousands of event planners around the country and we see that connection matters more than anything. Mentors help shine a light on alternative ways to do things. I have mentors in my life and I'm often asked to be a mentor as well. Recently I participated in a Mentor Day with a group of 17 professionals, and it's amazing how much we accomplished in a few hours and how we solved problems together.

When we are accepting new members in the Event Planners Club, we are looking for exceptional leaders who want to share resources and ideas with other members. They inspire others to be their best. When people ask who is an ideal member, I think of people who are creative, successful and amazing event planners along with vendors and suppliers who want to support leaders in the event planning space.

Which brings me to the question at the beginning of this chapter: why this book? We are publishing this book to share case studies and conversations we've been having with leaders in the community. This book taps into the genius that's in the community through those who have been highlighted to share their stories and what they have learned. The interviews allow us to really dig into issues facing people in our field and we share ways to overcome obstacles.

I personally got so much out of the interviews and I love the overflowing abundance of resources in this community.

Who should read this book? Entrepreneurs involved in the event planning industry along with professionals in the hotel industry, vendors in the event planning space and people who want to expand their knowledge of event planning. There are valuable golden nuggets in here that will help people create events that are memorable for themselves and for their clients as well.

Now is the time to start mining for gold and to create events that are unforgettable and meaningful for you and for your clients! I look forward to seeing your photos and hearing stories about your successful events!

"Dreaming is the most important thing we can all do. When you dream you have hope and you release the child inside you. And when your dreams come true, then you must always DREAM BIGGER."

BELIEVING
it's possible,
MAKES it
possible.

CHAPTER 2
David Tutera
Celebrity Wedding Planner

At the Event Planners Club, we identify what makes experts like David so unique. He's made a huge splash with big names, and built a brand around unforgettable celebrations.

EPC: David Tutera has been honored by Life and Style Magazine as the "Best Celebrity Wedding Planner". He's done weddings for J.Lo, Matthew McConaughey, Jewel, Star Jones, and Real Housewife Taylor Armstrong. He's done events at the White House. He's done post-Grammy parties in New York City. He's done events for Tommy Hilfiger and Susan Lucci. There's too many to name. He's also been on every TV show and media outlet known to man. Thank you so much for joining us. We know how valuable your time is. Let's go back in time a little bit. What inspired you to be in the event planning industry?

David: Oh wow, you know I wasn't really inspired to be in the industry. I've been doing this for so long that when I started, there really wasn't this go-to place to lean how to be an event planner or be a designer. I'd love to share with you the accidental process of how I got here.

EPC: That'd be great.

David: I was at Fordham University in New York City, and I

lived outside of New York City. Went to Fordham, left after a year and a half, answered an ad to make some money and I was the guy that dressed up in these embarrassing costumes and I would write songs to the recipient and go and sing them in these costumes, carrying balloons. It was a way of making money, and long story short, I opened up a teeny little store. I don't know if you know New York too well, but in the summer, there's a town called Larchmont, New York and it's an area that has money and they're the ones that spent 100-125 dollars back in 1986 to do singing telegrams. I had this little teeny store that I opened up after starting this out of my parent's home and someone came in my store and asked if I'd decorate their kid's bar mitzvah.

David: She said to me, "I have $2,500, will you decorate my son's bar mitzvah." I said, "Absolutely yes!" She laughed and then I called the one Jewish person I knew, "What the hell's a bar mitzvah?"

EPC: I love it.

David: I think about it ... I was 19; he was turning 13 so there was a six-year difference. He started me in this business of doing celebrations, to doing events.

EPC: You've got to track him down. You need a private eye or something.

David: I tried! It was funny, during a TV segment, we were trying to track him down but we couldn't find him. I remember his mother's name was Harriet, his name was Seth, and that's all I know.

EPC: So that was your first event. How do you go from $2,500 in 1986 decorating a bar mitzvah to J.Lo's wedding? And you've made yourself a household name, a meteoric rise.

David: I always try to share this with people in the industry. It is not an overnight success. It is an enormous amount of concentration, focus, failures, mistakes that you've listened and learned from. I took baby steps. I did little teeny parties for probably five years. My confidence is what sold me, not my expertise. I was smart enough in my own head to realize that not knowing what I'm doing meant I needed to have an enormous amount of confidence exuding from me.

EPC: That's a really good line.

David: It's true. I think there are people that are far more creative than I am. What I do best is I exude confidence and then I listen to people for what they're looking for, their expectations. My job is simply to be the carrier of bringing things to life. Somebody could make something much prettier than I can, but can I do it in a way that's exactly what the clients are looking for? I learned that from only working out of default. Someone saying, "I want a ceiling treatment for our celebration." Why do you need a ceiling treatment? You already have a ceiling in your room. Putting up flowers or fabric or realizing that there are these things that I never really knew. I didn't even know what a charger plate was, the show plate on a place setting. I had to teach myself these things, as my clients were far more educated in the world of entertaining than I'd ever been. I grew up with paper plates and brownies. That's how I grew up.

My form of education was my clients that paid me to do their jobs. It was fascinating. I grew in little baby steps. I went from being in Westchester County and never touching New York City to eventually segueing into Washington DC, to Atlanta, to Los Angeles, and then finally, finally feeling comfortable enough and more confident enough, to step into the arena of the socialites of New York City. That is a whole other world.

EPC: You mentioned taking baby steps, and some of the mistakes, and the things you learned along the way that helped you grow with each next event. What were some of the biggest lessons you learned?

David: Because I didn't know what was being asked of me, I always said yes and I did my homework after I got the job. Things were being presented to me, and I didn't even know what they were talking about. My job was always self-education. It was doing my homework. Listen, in 1986, you couldn't Google "What is this, and what is that?" You literally had to work harder to figure it out faster.

I'd have to say that I think listening and paying attention to your surroundings, joining associations - which was one of the things that really helped me the most. I remember joining almost every possible association out there. Going to cocktail parties, networking, learning from people that had been doing it far longer than I have. They actually knew what they were doing in the sense that they had a career. I was trying to create a career. Then you have to know when to dismiss yourself from it, to allow yourself to blossom.

EPC: That is awesome. What do you like best about what you do?

David: My job is different every day. I'm not that kind of person that could do the same thing every single day. I love making people happy, I love creating celebrations for anyone for any reason. Because I still do celebrations, I'm still an expert. I've built a brand through television, through books, through product lines. I think the most exciting part about it is now I have all this diversity going on, centralized around throwing celebrations.

EPC: What do you attribute your success to?

David: Standing out amongst the noise. Making sure that I'm a step ahead of everything else that's happening. This is an interesting industry. It's a copycat industry. Everyone loves to do what everybody else is doing, and I always love to create and run and let somebody else follow in my footsteps. I learned a long, long, long time ago, that the ideas I come up with, I don't want accolades and credit. I just want to do it fabulously, and then I want to move on and figure out something else that's different and new.

EPC: You talked about being original, which is obviously one way to stand out. What are some other ways you've used over the decades to stand out and position yourself differently from other celebration planners in the industry?

David: I think I knew when to take the next step. For example, here I am starting a company and creating a business, and then realizing back in 1999, 2000, I wanted to write a book. Chefs wrote books, nobody in the industry wrote an actual published book by a major publishing house. Then writing seven more books, and then getting on television and knowing that to get on TV, you need to have a book which is a calling card to be able to do a six-minute, five-minute segment to promote your book, which is promoting your brand, which is promoting what you do for a living, which is building the bigger brand, which is then allowing you to go out and say, "Hey, I've written seven books and I've produced events for all these great people. Now I want to create a product line." Then, you get to go out there and start that all over again. It's something to do with me always seeing where I am tomorrow as opposed to where I am today. Most people who get where they are today are very comfortable and confident. They get burned out doing the same thing, but they don't realize that there's a future ahead and something different for them, and they have to figure that out.

EPC: That is great advice. Let's sidetrack a little bit. Tell us about your passion for our furry friends.

David: I have two dogs. I have one new dog, if you don't know about our new dog. Teddy came into our little world two days before Christmas. Lucy came into my world, gosh, five years ago it's been. She was a rescue dog, but she was a stray, that came in. For those that don't know, I wasn't a dog person. I was absolutely petrified of dogs. When Lucy came into my life, it literally just changed that world. I fell in love with her. When I met Joey, my husband now, he had a very large dog, a Ridgeback. She joined our family, and since, she passed away a couple months ago. Then, I had a big, big dog with my small dog. Now, I was becoming very comfortable. Furry friends are now an extension to our life.

EPC: When you talk about celebrations, how do you measure a successful celebration?

David: Celebrations are not measured to me based on the amount of money people spent. Obviously that's important to me as a business owner, but celebrations that are successful are when you look around a room and you have guests not wanting to leave the celebration, smiling and detaching from their everyday life, being part of something they weren't expecting to be part of, and coming over to me as their planner and designer and say, "Thank you for creating this moment." Celebrations - weddings, bar mitzvahs, anniversaries, whatever the event is, they're the same every day. There are just so many ways you can turn it for a wedding. There are so many different ways you can create a six-hour celebration.

What I do is I flip it all around and I create moments for people who become interactive participants, as opposed to passive. They're realizing that they're on this journey that I've created for my client and for the guests. That, to me, is the most gratifying.

EPC: With all the amazing success you've achieved, what's your biggest challenge now?

David: I think my biggest challenge is to continue to build the brand, to continue to bring products and solutions to people. I'm obsessed with finding unique, creative things that don't exist, which is hard because so much is out there, and developing it, producing it, getting it on shelves, meeting with manufacturers, meeting with retailers, meeting with the consumers. As you know, I'm coming over the flu I just had after three weeks of traveling around the country meeting people. My job is to be very present. It's easy to say you're an expert and a celebrity, and just stay at home and not do much, but I'm out in the field. I'm listening, I'm learning, I'm sharing, I'm teaching, I'm educating, I'm part of it. That's what makes it exciting for me.

EPC: Now you've also given back a lot. You've also done a lot of work in the celebration industry, helping other event planners. Celebration coordinators learn from some of the success you've achieved. Talk a little bit about your different ventures in that department, and how our event planners can take advantage of some of those and start learning from you.

David: It's one of my most favorite things to do, to get in front of an audience and teach. I don't like to say that I'm on a pedestal teaching down because of my experience. I'm always trying to explain to people that I'm a messenger. I can guide and direct you and give you advice, but my advice might not be right for that particular person. I started the *David Tutera Symposium* last year and it's one of my favorite things because it's a very intimate group of people.

It's three days of events. The evenings are filled with celebrations, but most importantly, the days are filled with education. I'm the keynote speaker, I'm your moderator throughout. There are experts at every field imaginable that can really walk you through the things you need to learn and build your business. We are

16

teaching people how to be creative. People that are planners are not necessarily creative. People that are designers are not necessarily planners. We're trying to bridge the two worlds, to give them the best of both. At the end of the symposium, two people will be selected based upon their growth over the three days and they will have the opportunity to come work for me, on a project, a big event, and they will literally get paid, work for me as a David Tutera employee, and learn how to really do it the big way.

EPC: You've written seven books. Tell us a little bit about your writing.

David: I do it in a comical way. My writing is a little bit tongue in cheek. I learned that too many people in this business of entertaining take it too seriously. It's important to take your business seriously. I don't believe it's important to take yourself seriously. It's a big difference.

When I write, I write with humor because I feel when people are stressed as planners or designers, and they're dealing with clients that are very stressed and emotional, our job is to keep it light. Make light of it, make a joke of it, make some sort of simple comparison to something that's light and not related to what we're specifically talking about. You find that in my writing because, not to use this common phrase, we are creating events, we're not curing and fixing the world. I think too many people too often now in this business have taken it so seriously that they just simply don't know how to chill out.

EPC: That is an excellent, excellent point. For our event planners who want to be more like David when they grow up, what is the best place for them to learn more about you?

David: If they go to https://davidtutera.com/, it will take you to the *David Tutera Event Planning Symposium*. It will walk you through finding out about my books, and where I'm doing appearances, and you can learn about my product lines. I think it's the go-to hub, which is basically my name, dot-com. It'll share with people what's happening in my life. Social media for me is a massive outlet, from Facebook to Twitter to Instagram to Pinterest and everything else that's been added on. There's probably a new social media outlet since we've been speaking.

I share a lot there. I share a lot of things that I do, both personally, and professionally. I enjoy doing that because I'm very grateful for the fans that have watched me on television. They've allowed me to build a business. I always feel it's important for me to share with them the new things that are happening, and the questions I have for them in hopes they can answer for me to give me some direction.

EPC: Absolutely. We are incredibly grateful for you to spend time with us. They will be super excited to know that they're going to get the chance to learn more from you. David, thank you so much for joining us.

David: You're welcome. It was a pleasure.

EPC Book Recommendation:

David's Book, *My Fair Wedding: Finding Your Vision...Through His Revisions!*

CHAPTER 3
Andrea Adelstein
NYLUX Events

At the Event Planners Club, we identify what makes experts like Andrea so unique. She creates family members at milestone events. This drives her high referral rate.

EPC: Andrea Adelstein of nyluxevents.com is sharing her secrets of special family milestone experiences.

Andrea: Thank you so much!

EPC: What inspired you to get in the event planning industry?

Andrea: I grew up in a family that entertained all the time. When I was 10 years old, my mom went into the invitation business. Then later on, one of my close friends became an event planner and it really excited me.

EPC: How did you get to this point in your career?

Andrea: There were three key stages. Initially I was working for my friend's event planning business. Initially I'd do on-site work for specific events, and then started leading smaller pieces of the events which led me to work with him full time. Then I transitioned to work for a well-known event planner, Claudia Glenn, from Claudia Glenn Events. After many years together, we became event partners. We did all sorts of fantastic events. Then ultimately, I established my own events business and Claudia and I formed a partnership. It's been great.

EPC: Do you have a specific area of event-planning expertise? If so, what is it?

Andrea: Actually we, Claudia and I, really pride ourselves in doing all sorts of different kinds of events. We're not solely one kind of planner. I think, for us, it really is terrific because everything becomes fresh and new and exciting, even though there definitely is a level of "this is what you do" each time, and there's a time line that we follow with all events. Everything becomes new and fresh and creative. We do weddings. We do bar mitzvahs. We do a lot of what we call milestone events, things that are really important to families. Last year I think we did a 45th, a 60th, a 65th, and a 70th birthday celebration. Those are completely different than the bar and bat mitzvahs, which we do quite a few annually.

We just did a 60th wedding anniversary, which is incredible. Next week, we're in LA. We're doing a three-day conference at the Beverly Hills Hilton. There are two-night events and then we're running a whole lounge all day, during the day, with exciting things going on. We really pride ourselves in being able to give our clients the party that they want. It's not very formulaic from a creative point of view. It's great and I love it. I wouldn't really have it any other way.

EPC: What are some of the biggest event planning mistakes you see clients making and how do you help them avoid those or solve them?

Andrea: Clients sometimes get bogged down in very small details and miss big pictures. I've had clients focus on one or two pieces of small décor, something that goes hanging over a bar, and they're hyper-focused on it, and they avoid doing seating. To me, seating is one of the things that makes your party fantastic. If your guests are seated at a table with people that they want to talk to, find interesting, then they're going to have a fantastic time at your party, regardless of what piece of décor is hanging over the bar. That's really one key thing is getting bogged down in small details and not seeing the big picture.

Another one is not putting enough stock in lighting. Everybody's very big on centerpieces, but if I had only a limited budget, I would light the place liberally, and be creative in an inexpensive centerpiece, and yet clients really do focus on the centerpiece sometimes really more than they should. Those two things are really key.

Especially in places like New York, Chicago, LA, where we do work, people don't realize the dollars that go in just for food and catering and venue space, so they have this budget that they think is going to go so far, but in all of those cities, food is expensive. They don't realize that their budget doesn't always accommodate their guest list and the way they want it to lay out. Those would be three things that I find are common, across-the-board mistakes. We just work with them patiently and explain, show pictures, give examples, and help them understand, so that they feel really comfortable with what we're doing, and they get the event that they see in their head and are happy with the outcome.

One of the things that we find we have to do, and it's related to your question, is manage expectations. A lot of people have very big expectations for a party that they've been looking forward to for many, many years, especially if it's a wedding, and their expectations don't always work with their budget. Their expectations are not realistic for execution in the time frame that we have to set up the space. They may like it for themselves, but it doesn't always work with their guests. We really manage clients' expectations, because when they understand what they're getting, they're happier with the end result.

EPC: That makes a lot of sense. How do you measure a successful event?

Andrea: I think in different ways. One is knowing that we put together the best possible event that we could in the time frame and with the budget that we allow. The pulse of the evening, we always know when it's a little slow and we adjust. We know when it's fantastic. Then of course, based on how the client is feeling and all of the afterglow. Then you know how you've really scored. Happily, we've scored a lot lately. I'm really proud and happy about that.

EPC: That makes a lot of sense. What do you like best about your business?

Andrea: There's a lot of things. I love working with people. I love the idea of, in this very busy world, being able to share with them and help them get joy out of a lot of their events. I find that sometimes, some of these events, really bring families together that sometimes were struggling, and watch people's families who live very far away from each other come together for a weekend and love it and have a wonderful time. In the end, those are the memories everybody has. That's why we work hard, so we can be together and enjoy and relax. If I can help facilitate that, then that's fantastic.

EPC: Absolutely. What do you attribute your success to?

Andrea: I think that event planning is a three-prong business. I think recognizing that helps me be successful. Those three pieces are being creative, and I believe that I am myself, and we are as a team, very creative, and we have wonderful ideas and exciting things. I think we're very organized and we help people manage their time well and they're very appreciative of being able to go through planning these events and having them planned so that they're calm and relaxed and enjoying it.

Then we spend a lot of time with the families. There's a piece of event planning that I think is very much being a best friend. We get involved in their families and we talk them through it. We help them see other people's positions. I think people really enjoy having a third person explain things. It's made us very successful. We have a policy that we never raise our voice. We don't say a bad thing. We really go into this with a positive outlook and attitude. I think clients really respond well and we get most of our business from referrals. We've been successful and I know clients are happy, because they're referring us. It's made us successful, being nice.

EPC: Being nice is a marketing strategy.

Andrea: Yeah. Actually, with clients, it is. I think the days of telling clients what they have to have in demanding way, and there was a time when that's the way planners worked, it doesn't really work anymore. People want to be treated well. They're spending a lot of money. There are nice ways to say, "No. You can't do that." I think if you can do that, you become successful.

EPC: I would agree. With all the success you've achieved, what is your biggest challenge now?

Andrea: Growing the business is definitely a challenge. We're looking forward to doing more business in LA. Claudia, my partner, is now in LA. We have somebody in Chicago, so we're really looking to expand in those areas. We've started to do work in Florida and Austin. It's a challenge to develop resources in all of those areas, become experts in those areas, so that we can give the level of service that we can locally, in New York, in the Hamptons, and the whole metro area. We can give that level of service in those new places and that takes time and energy and resources, patience. We're really working on those areas as our next growth spot.

EPC: What challenges do you face when sourcing entertainment for your clients?

Andrea: I think that entertainment is something that everybody doesn't understand what goes into it to get the result that they want. They don't understand always, that you need to pay for groups' rehearsal fees. You need to light the groups well. You need separate sound systems and all of that. It's about explaining and teaching and having them understand and playing different kinds of music for them, samples, so that they get an idea. Again, I really believe in this. Education is the way to being successful. When I sit down and explain and show pictures and examples and play music for them, they really do understand why they need to spend what they need to spend or why they can't have what they were thinking.

EPC: That makes a lot of sense. How do you evaluate potential vendors to use for your clients?

Andrea: We never use new vendors that we haven't gone through a little bit of a search process. We call around and see who's used them before, by talking to other resources. We check their website. We like to go and meet them. I've had lunch with lots and lots of different entertainment vendors before we sign them up. I want to see how they speak, how they look, how they feel about their job. I want to get to know them, because I want to have faith that they're going to do what they say they're going to do, they're going to be professional at all of our events, and they will give me the result that I need.

          I'm entrusting a piece of my event to them and there's nothing worse than having a vendor who doesn't show up on time, look right, and certainly provide what we've paid them in advance for. I'm very, very good about paying everybody either early or on time, and I think the vendors always appreciate that. They know that they're definitely getting paid and they're getting paid for their work. They're getting paid timely. We work together with them really closely, but we vet them before we use them. We do a lot of research. If it's music, we listen to a lot of samples of theirs. We're very, very careful, because they can make or break a party. Our reputation is based on our recommendations and that's really important.

EPC: Absolutely. How do you manage the financial aspects of your business?

Andrea: Thankfully, we have somebody who helps us, because planning and doing paperwork is always a challenge in your day. We are careful with how we price everything. We want our clients to feel good about what they pay, but we also believe all of our vendors need to be paid properly for their services. Then, of course, we want to make money. We are very thoughtful. We have a lot of conversation about pricing, always, and what we get for our money. I really feel that that is the key. Regardless of what a client wants to spend, they need to get a lot for their money, and we need to control the pricing versus what is delivered. We're careful about what we charge and what we feel is fair all the way around.

EPC: Anything drive you crazy about your business?

Andrea: Yes. Competition, where clients are very

competitive about where they're looking at different people's events, and they want what somebody else has, but that doesn't necessarily mean it's in their budget. The internet drives me bonkers in this business, because I could be proposing certain things of décor and then I have clients call me up and say they saw it online for X price, but when you start to explain to them it's not the right color and it's not the right size and it needs to be put together, which you have to pay somebody to put it together, again, it's patience and educating them.

The internet, Pinterest, drives me nuts, because people bring me pictures of things that they would like to have that they have no idea how long it takes to put it together, how many pieces put those puzzles together, how expensive it is, the weight of the paper. They don't understand lots of the pieces, but they wave around pictures and say, "I want this. I want this." I'm like, "You can have it, if you want to triple your invitation budget. I'm happy to give it to you." We sit down, and I say, "We can do it this way, or we can do it that way. You can have the same feeling or effect, but not the same thing." People don't relate to what they see and the costs. The internet has just opened the world up for creativity, but in some ways, it's driving us all a little mad.

EPC: Who is an ideal client for you?

Andrea: An ideal client? Oh, we just had an ideal client, it was a 60th wedding anniversary. She was fantastic. She knew what she wanted. They knew where they wanted to have it and they really had fantastic priorities. They spent an enormous amount of time really seating their guests, talking about the guest list, who they wanted, how they wanted the tables assorted, where the tables should be, so that everybody could meet somebody new, spend time with somebody that they might find interesting. They even joked that they might even get a wedding out of it, by sitting some people next to each other.

Their priorities really were entertaining their guests with great entertainment and food, and they were less bogged down in the little details of escort cards, or this color fuchsia versus that hue of fuchsia. They wanted it beautiful. They let us do our job, which is fantastic, and they were focused on really giving their guests a fantastic night, and celebrating their family, which was also a priority. They trusted us. When you have a client like that, we gave them 150 percent. We so enjoyed working with them. They loved so much that we gave them, and when they wanted it different, we were happy to go out and do whatever would make them happy, because they were pleasant and fun. They had a phenomenal event. It was just amazing to work on. It was this past October. It was spectacular.

EPC: It sounds it. What is the first step you would want that ideal client to take to start engaging with you?

Andrea: That's a great question. To start engaging with us, I like to meet clients in their home. I like to sit with them in their home and have them talk about what they want from the evening. What are their priorities? Is it to bring the family together? Is it to entertain their guests with phenomenal food or

30

phenomenal entertainment? I need them to really be thoughtful about what is this event and what does it mean to them? From there, it really helps us give them what they want. Going to their home really helps a lot as well, because everybody uses the same words, like contemporary or classic or warm or rustic, but my rustic isn't necessarily my client's rustic. When I go to their home and we start talking about things, and I can ask them about their taste, it really helps me hone in on what they want. The client needs to be focused in some ways, because they know that they want an anniversary party, or they know that they want this type of wedding, but I want them to be open to new ideas as well. They can contact me at andrea@nyluxevents.com.

EPC: That is a good answer.

Andrea: Thank you so much!

EPC Book Recommendation:

Birthday Guest Book: Celebrating 70 Years

Remember...
You are
Capable of
AMAZING
things!

CHAPTER 4
June Archer
Speaker/Author/Coach

At the Event Planners Club, we identify what makes experts like June so unique. He is big Hollywood, but is grounded in charity events.

EPC: June Archer is an author, motivational speaker, and has his own entertainment company.

Let's go back in time. Where did you grow up?

June: I'm originally from Hartford, Connecticut. Born in Hartford and raised in a small town called Windsor, Connecticut, where I realized that dreams do come true. I was a young kid that wanted to sing and dance like Michael Jackson and had the great opportunity and was blessed to get a record deal in 1995 with a bunch of childhood friends of mine, and signed a recording contract with Electric Records back in the day. Had the opportunity to be a boy band, we were a boy band in the 90s. That's how I got on my path of music and entertainment, and at that point, I realized I really loved this thing called entertainment. I love getting people together, so it was a way for me to get people together, have a good time, and really start what I now know as a viable business to entertain people.

EPC: That is awesome. That's what inspired you. How did

you go from getting a record deal to what you're doing now?

June: What I'm doing now is, I've become now an author and motivational speaker. I'll take a few steps back and tell you the story that at one point, the music just started to sound different and things just started to be different. For us, we lost our record deal two years in because it was just too much, too fast, too soon. We saw our names and our songs on the charts and saw ourselves on MTV, BET, VH1, when they actually played videos.

Going back, and heard our record on the radio and saw ourselves in magazines, and it was just so much. To be so young and have your dreams realized, and sometimes people say, be careful what you ask for, you just might get it. That was a classic case of getting exactly what it is that you prayed for and not being able to handle it. From there, I just realized that my dreams weren't over. I had more dreams in me. I took that celebrity and I said, I want to start events. I want to do events.

I started raising money for AIDS and breast cancer for my birthday called the June Archer Celebration of Life, where every year, Thanksgiving weekend, I would raise money. We've had upwards of twelve hundred people in one night participate and have a good time. I would have fashion show and DJ party, band, auction, and raise money to send over to Uganda, Africa, for clinics that were reusing needles and didn't have alcohol, and didn't have latex gloves, and syringes, so money from the event would go to that, and it was also building awareness for breast cancer, as well as the AIDS piece of it. I realized that people really love my events and I really dove into event planning and doing events, and helping to market and promote other peoples' events, and kind of tagging myself with what they're doing, and kind of help them build their brand in terms of what they're doing in terms of their events. Whether it was a jazz festival, whether it was a wine tasting, or a book signing, and just realize that I had this influence in my community to actually get people out, to come and actually support an author or an artist. It's been a great thing.

From there, I started writing posts on Facebook and just giving people words of encouragement. Until one day, people just kept saying, hey, you should write a book. Long story short, I ended up putting all these quotes into a book form and created this book called "Yes, Every Day Can Be a Good Day: The Keys to Success that Lead to an Amazing Life" and it's been taking me around the country for the past two-and-a-half years.

EPC: That is absolutely an incredible journey, and if it hasn't already, that story should fill a book. Do you have a certain type of event you like to work on the most?

June: I like charitable events. Only because it's putting sugar in the medicine. Some people, they want to give back, but if it's too mundane, if it's too boring, they won't come and they won't support it. If you kind of throw an event where you just put the sugar in the medicine, have a DJ, have a nice band, and have them make a donation at the door, they realize that they're coming to start the party with a purpose. You come, and those kinds of events, I love because you get to network. You get to listen to music. You get to meet new people. Those are my favorite events, especially music events, where we have live entertainment because I come from the music side. For me, to merge all of those worlds together is a beautiful thing. Now, I love merging food and entertainment with hospitality and really just making some magic happen.

EPC: Of course. How do you measure a successful event?

June: The way to measure an event is the takeaway. We have this thing called social media, right now, and if you can have people speak about your event after the event, I think you become very successful. If there is a takeaway that allows them to take action at the event, you become successful. If they're having fun at the event, and you give them the hashtag, and you give them those key words for the event and you see that it's trending, even if it's on the small level, I think you can say, you know what? This was a very successful event. It's not just monetary. Money comes and goes. Just because you don't make a lot of money from your event doesn't mean it won't be successful. It's the action after the event. What kind of impact did you leave the consumer or the patron after they attended the event?

EPC: I think that's a great way to measure it. What do you like best about your business?

June: Meeting people. Meeting new people every day. It never gets old. I am one, I never forget a face. Names, you know, I think I need a new hard drive in my head. I've met a lot of people on this journey, however, I never forget a face and to meet someone and have an interaction with them, and you realize that the world becomes so much smaller when you meet more people, that you become to build this network of people that, no matter where you are in the country, no matter where you are in the world, you can make dots connect because along this journey, you've met so many people. I think, they say you increase your net worth by building your network. I think you increase and build your network as you network because once you become the common denominator, you become the person that is valuable because you have the relationships.

For me, I want to meet as many people as I can. Whether they're of value or not, whether they can do something for me or not because I've learned, if you're not being used, you're being useless. Some people look at it as, he only calls when he wants something. He only calls if he needs me to connect at such-and-such, if he needs a resource for this. If Seth doesn't call you, you are nonexistent. If he calls you, even if it's for a favor, even if it's to connect you with something, you are the common denominator, you are resourceful. That means you are powerful. If you can connect dots, you are powerful. You know how much people would pay for that kind of influence?

EPC: I think there are a couple writer-downers in what you said and a couple quotable things, at least. You've had such an interesting journey. What do you attribute your success to?

June: Learning to live good with people. Just making sure that whatever it is that you're putting out into the universe, whatever you're putting out into the community, that you stand behind that. You are your brand. A lot of people, we take this thing brand, we take this word brand and we just throw it around, right? But you have to realize that you're more than one brand, and you're always creating a brand for yourself because whatever your parents' last name is, you carry that brand. You carry that brand because it's your last name, but you also carry the brand of whatever it is that is your business. That is your business card. That is your calling card.

When you step out of the house, you have to be able to walk with purpose and understanding that you create more business on how you act and treat others. If others feel like you don't treat them well, the whole word of mouth piece for you and your business, and growing organically is out the window. You have to work that much harder to prove to people hey, you visit me, you can trust me, I'm a nice guy. But if you have to say all of that, then you're already in the deficit.

EPC: Absolutely. That is so important. With all the success that you've achieved, what's your biggest challenge now?

June: The biggest challenge right now is to sustain what I have and continue to build this business, and juggle so many things because some of my mentors, and some of them don't know that they're my mentors. When you talk about the Oprah Winfrey's of the world. When you look at someone like a Russell Simmons or a Jay-Z, or Tony Robbins is up there as well. They have multiple businesses. They have multiple streams of revenue, and if they can do it. A lot of people say, and I think it's a disservice to our young people, oh, just focus on one thing. Focus on that one thing and be good at that one thing. That's great, but what about the young person, such as myself that I have to do more than one thing. I want to conquer everything.

I am now an author, I'm now a motivational speaker who people are calling on to speak about everything from motivation, inspiration to diversity inclusion, to motivating their employees to motivating their students, to still being in the music business, working on music for everybody from Jay-Z to Beyoncé to Jennifer Hudson, to also marketing and promoting people's events. To also doing the social media marketing for businesses that are looking to make sure that their digital real estate out there on the social media platforms exist and is working, and allowing them to have people come back to their website to be able to push their products, their goods, and their services. For me, it's "How do I sustain it, how do I build more businesses, get more streams of revenue in, but also, how do I change the world?" That's most important.

EPC: How do I change the world, I love that. When you're producing these events, how do you determine what vendors to use? How do you evaluate them?

June: I evaluate how they treat people, regardless of the event that I have there. If they are a location and a business that people truly love, what I have is value. I'm bringing value to your establishment. If I'm bringing you twelve hundred paying customers, you want them to be successful long after you're gone, as well, right? If you give me the opportunity to make sure that these patrons have a great experience, they'll come back way after the event that I do and they'll come back, and they'll purchase whatever that you're selling. They'll come back and they'll buy your food, they'll come back and have a drink at your establishment, based on the experience that they had when we worked together.

I look for people who really have a hold on the community, who do good business, and can allow me to help me make magic happen, and at the end of the day, they can have new business based on what I've done, and I can say we had a great event, and people walk away and say, hey, do you remember that event at such-and-such a place when June did it? I still go back there. For me, that's the more important piece as to who I tend to work with over the years. I tend to be very particular and very loyal because you continue to create magic and you grow together. You grow your businesses and your brands together, so for me that's important that we all become successful together.

EPC: Absolutely. That makes a lot of sense. How do you differentiate yourself from other folks who might be producing similar types of events?

June: I keep my head down. I always have been of the thought that you can't have McDonald's without Burger King. You can't have Coke without Pepsi, right? I've been doing my Celebration of Life event for 20 years. No one else has been doing it on Thanksgiving weekend. It's kind of like everyone knows, don't throw an event Thanksgiving weekend, that's June Archer's weekend. There are people who have events the weekend before, the weekend after, not as big, but it always allows me to kind of see what the community is looking for. If I can't be the first to do it, be the first to do it the way I do it. My hot chocolate soul event, which is music, comedy, and poetry. Twenty years this year. I've been doing it consistently that even when someone comes in, I love the competition, so it allows me to up the ante doing what I do, and making more magic happen, and pull some rabbits out of my hat.

I kind of look at what's going on. I keep my head down. I look at the bigger picture. I look at what people on television are doing, you know? What is Ryan Seacrest doing? That's my competition, even though it's on a much larger scale because when I get to that point where I'm able to compete with the Simon Cowells or the Ryan Seacrests, guys that are having these shows on television, I have the mindset that I can be that successful, but I have to work hard. I've done it on a small scale, and I've done it for twenty years, that because I'm so competitive, I know I can compete on that level.

EPC: For our folks who are resonating with what you're saying and want to learn more about you, what is the best place for them to go?

June: Best place to find me is on my website IamJuneArcher.com. If you want to follow me, I am on every social media platform, @JuneArcher. Everything is @JuneArcher. I'm doing this thing, Monday through Friday. I take the weekends to have family time, but I'm on my social media platforms, pushing positivity, motivation, helping people realize their dreams, as well as making sure that anyone that comes to any of my events, they have a great time, they walk away with something, they feel special, and the call to action is to change the world.

EPC: I absolutely love it. Fascinating interview, incredible story. Thank you so much, we greatly appreciate it.

EPC Book Recommendation:

June's book, *Yes, Every Day Can Be a Good Day: The Keys to Success that Lead to an Amazing Life*

Take time
to do what
makes you
happy.

CHAPTER 5
Christy Bareijsza
Events by Red Carpet

At the Event Planners Club, we identify what makes
experts like Christy so unique. She's a big market player in
NYC, Miami, LA and SF, and is available to clients 24/7.
Now that's red carpet service.

EPC: Christy Bareijsza, the owner of Red Carpet Events, has built an amazing business.

Christy: Thank you, I enjoy sharing what I've learned.

EPC: Let's go back in time a little bit. What inspired you to be in the event planning industry?

Christy: What inspired me? I was working in New York City at a company called Chase and completely miserable opening checking accounts, working in a branch and didn't realize that this was what real life was about. They had a job that was an event coordinator position. It was something that I just felt like I would be inspired by. I thought it was fun. I thought it would be entertaining and I tried to apply for it and they wouldn't let me do it because I was so low on the totem pole. Basically, what I did at that point was I went back to school at NYU. They have a great event planning and management program and I actually went and got a degree in meeting and event management and then called a recruiter and actually began my career as a meeting planner.

It was something to the effect of being told "Hey, you can't do it." So, I said, "All right, I'm going to do it." That's how I ended up in the career. From there I became a meeting planner for Young then Oppenheimer Funds and then I was running the event department for TD Ameritrade for years. Went to Barclays and got some international experience and then finally went on my own at the end of 2005 so it kind was a, I guess, quick progression but definitely just continued on doing those things that I love.

EPC: Awesome. How did you get from there to the Red Carpet Events?

Christy: I just quit my job basically. It was one of those things that I started my company in 2001 part time as an entity where I figured at some point in time I would end up being on my own. I'm a child of entrepreneurs so it was in my blood and after having the corporate experience and really understanding how the big companies work, I had built up my company little by little and then in the end of 2005 I was just done and I quit my job and I said, "I'm going to do this". I did it and I never looked back. Some people think you're crazy for jumping with two feet in but sometimes it's the best way to do it because you just have to swim.

EPC: Congratulations. That is an incredible story. Tell us about some of the distinct types of events you produce.

Christy: We do everything from corporate to social events. A whole gambit of meetings, conferences, pop up events. I've done my occasional wedding. I don't have a lot of patience for weddings, but I will do them. We do extraordinary events, galas, recognition dinners, incentive conferences. You name it, we've pretty much done it. We always say yes because you never know what this one piece of business is going to lead to the next and who's there and who's going to be watching you.

EPC: What have been some of the biggest event planning mistakes you've seen clients make and how did you help them fix that?

Christy: They think that they can Google it and they're event planners. My favorite line is, you're not going to go into surgery with a doctor and say, "Well I did a search on Google for this, so I know how to perform surgery." A lot of times we have a little bit of a battle of wills with the clients because they feel as though they've planned their own wedding, they've planned their child's birthday, they've planned a sorority dinner and now suddenly, they're event planners. We try to instill our processes and get them to understand that we have these certain things in place like production schedules and accountability with the vendors and the follow up and the different communication methods to ensure their events run flawlessly.

Sometimes they will eventually give in and let us know and understand that we are here to help them, and we are the experts in the industry and we're not here to take the credit. We're here to make sure that they look fabulous. Sometimes too we've got to let them make those mistakes too because then we get the phone call back. It's a different kind of respect and it's a different type of relationship after that too because they realize that when it looks easy it's because we made it look easy, not because it is easy.

EPC: That is an excellent point. How do you measure a successful event?

Christy: Well we've got the famous three letters, the return on investment, the ROI. It depends on what the client is. We just had a client were we did national road shows for them and their sales and their attendance went up well over 65 percent. That's black and white and cut and dry. We have another client that we'll do these grand openings for them and when their membership sales increase substantially that's a return on investment. But we have the other events, where it's not so sales related where it's that stress relief, that smile on their face, that feeling that they really enjoyed the evening. That's also a success for us too. As well as creating a memory in people's minds that they had this great night or great day or great week-long experience that will be everlasting for them so there's different forms of it but as long as it's achieved it's a success for us.

EPC: What do you like best about what you do?

Christy: It's got a start and a finish to it. You've got the project's beginning and there's sometimes stress at times and there's a lot of different things going on all at once so it's the fact that you're always juggling multiple balls at once. When it's complete there's just this feeling of excitement and relief but it's one of those things that with each project it's unique, it's custom, it's different, it's new and there's always a different experience. It never gets old and it never gets boring.

EPC: Never gets old, never gets boring. I think that's a great writer downer right there. What do you attribute your success to?

Christy: Hard work is one of them. I think also, with that hard work, it's your reputation because that's all you have. It's maintaining good vendors. Maintaining loyalty. As an event planner you're not doing this by yourself and anyone who says they're doing it by themselves isn't doing it at all. You must have a talented team behind you and people that support you because not every event is going to have the biggest budget. Not every event is going to be the most exciting event. It's taking the big with the small. Always looking at opportunities as it can lead into something else.

Just keeping an open positive mind that this might be a little difficult step or business might be slow or business might be hectic but it's going to lead into something else. That's what makes the profession fun because you could get a phone call tomorrow next thing you know you're producing an amazing event and it's because that person went to one of your events six years ago. It's always that anticipation for a new surprise, which is a pleasant surprise. Those are the good surprises to have.

49

Unpleasant surprises are when something happens at the event that you weren't participating, but these kinds of surprises are good surprises.

EPC: Very true. With all the success you've achieved what would you say is your biggest challenge now?

Christy: The economy. That's the biggest challenge. I can't control it. We're in an election year this year. When you are in an election year people don't know what party is going to be in office next, so they tend to pull back on budget. They tend to pull back on making decisions. They tend to pull back on being a little bit more lavish, exposed with any type of event that they're doing. It's one of those things where it's hard for us to control because it is the economy and there's only so much we can do about it so how we can weather it is by diversifying our business a little bit further and making sure that we are weathering the storm because we had to weather it the last 10 years with the economy going up and down in a roller coaster. You just try to learn from those lessons and ensure that it doesn't happen so extreme the second time around or the third time around. Because it will always continue to happen. It'll happen every four years. That's one of the major, major factors.

EPC: What challenges do you face when you're sourcing entertainment for your clients?

Christy: Attitude. Diva-ness. We deal with a lot of celebrity talents, so my clients are always usually looking for the most popular person or the biggest celebrity. Me personally I'm looking for the person that's not going to drive us insane, that's going to be at a sound check on time and ensure that they meet and greet the VIPs and really give the client a value for what they just paid because usually it's an exorbitant amount. Some of those things, keeping people on time and making sure that they're doing what they have agreed to do via contract is one of those huge crucial factors with dealing with talent. Talking with the client and really communicating with them and making sure that they're booking the right talent that is going to give them the experience that they want.

EPC: I think that makes a lot of sense. How do you evaluate vendors to serve at your events? I know you talked about part of that but any other factors that might come into play?

Christy: You know the biggest thing is the response time. That's always an initial indication because if I am going to be paying a vendor, I shouldn't have to send you more than one email. I shouldn't have to follow up multiple times to get a bid. I shouldn't have to ask for changes or concessions multiple times. I think it's the initial relationship on whether you're going to mesh right away is crucial and then because it's the beginning of a relationship. That's going to really set the standard on what it's going to be two, three, four years down the line. If it's rocky in the beginning that's usually a big red flag.

Going forward with that it's also the reputation. I mean I'm not a big advocate of reading reviews on Yelp and things like that because they're not necessarily the most valid because you don't know

51

what kind of experience and they could have been a guest at the event versus another planner, but I will always take a recommendation from a colleague just because they also understand different points that we might be looking for in a vendor. If the relationship doesn't start out right, it usually never gets better so what you see in the beginning. There's so many great vendors out there, you just need to weed out the bad ones and find the good ones.

EPC: Who is an ideal client for you?

Christy: Corporations. We like them. I'm a very black and white person and they tend to be equally as black and white where we have a budget. This is what the numbers are. We can break down the numbers and this is what we can do, this is what we can't do. This is how we can maintain the budget. Also, too they tend to do more full events. We can do a variety of events. Some clients we have that's corporate can do a meeting to conference to next thing they're launching a product so they're going to do a special event or they're going to do a gala dinner. Maybe they've ended up sponsoring some type of film festival, so they might do a hospitality suite in that. It offers ups a variety of experiences as well as most corporations tend to understand and value event planners a little differently because they know it's a necessity. They know that we're going to be able to negotiate savings for them. We are going to be able to have accountable vendors and negotiate concessions for them too.

We can go above and beyond the call of duty as well as too we don't want their job. I love what I do. I'm not trying to go back into a corporate capacity so we're here to make them look great to their managers and their executive team, so they tend to respect what our roles are a lot better as well as they maintain loyalty which is great for us too. We really go to bat for our clients and we love that they appreciate that too.

EPC: Absolutely. What is the first step you would want someone interested in using your services to take?

Christy: I want them to research us. I want them to see what we do. I want them to look at our website and see the other events that we've done as well as be comfortable with it because when you're selling a service, most people don't understand that you're really buying into the team and you're buying into the person to be your onsite manager from start to finish. It's not like you're walking into a dealership and buying a car where you if you touch it, feel it, drive it, look at it, back it up but it's something that is a service. I want them to understand us and understand the methodologies that we use. We're a company that really gets down to business.

I've got four offices in New York, LA, Miami, and San Francisco. Each clientele is a little bit different, but they understand that they're always going to get a response time instantly. We're a seven-day a week company. You can call me on Sunday. We're going to answer the phone because we're going to get it done because we believe in that type of service. They need to understand that from the beginning and then they're going to understand the difference between events that are Red Carpet versus other companies and hopefully they'll see that right in the beginning. When we start talking about pricing and budgets and things like that it's a better understanding and there's no surprises.

EPC: You mentioned offices in multiple cities. How many event planners do you have working for you now?

Christy: I have one in each office, but we have a lot of contractors so when we do the larger events where we need a team of thirty, we have them. We try to keep things small because our events range from ten people to five thousand people so based on what it is we tend to keep our overhead as low as possible to keep our costs down and to keep the client costs down and then from there we make the decisions based on what the perimeters of the event are.

EPC: How many events do your four offices do every year?

Christy: Well we have a range of large to smaller events. We tend to do between 30 and 50 events a year. Some of them may be very small dinners to large grand openings with 500, 600 people to a huge event with a top name celebrity where we might have 5,000 people. It really ranges in what it is. With our business it's not necessarily the quantity, it's the quality of the event and that's the most important thing.

EPC: Anything you want to share?

Christy: I think it's, when you look for an event planner and you look for a company and you talk to an entrepreneur you really want to find someone that loves what they do. I think that's one of the most important things as well as having the educational background to really understand what your needs are because you might be dealing with strike and labor issues, you might be dealing with an additional contract negotiation, addendums. There's different key factors to really understanding the difference in a company because a lot of times people will see a great planner on TV or they'll see an advertisement and think that that's what makes them great. It's so much more than that and you know, yes, that's what we hope that people see the difference.

EPC: Christy from theredcarpetevents.com. Thank you so much for sharing your secrets

Christy: It's a pleasure. Take care.

EPC: Thanks so much.

EPC Book Recommendation:

501 Ways to Roll Out the Red Carpet for Your Customers: Easy-to-Implement Ideas to Inspire Loyalty, Get New Customers, and Make a Lasting Impression by Donna Cutting

---

An event EXPERIENCE activates all 5 senses!

CHAPTER 6
Jack Farmer
DJ Jack Farmer

At the Event Planners Club, we identify what makes experts like Jack so unique. He measures success by the strength of the Groom's thank you hug and the Bride's happy tears.

EPC: Thank you so such for joining us today, Jack Farmer of DJ Jack Farmer. How did you get started?

Jack: Funny enough I started because I just needed a way to pay my bills, while I was going to school. As I was looking for jobs I stumbled across a DJ Company who was trying to hire a Warehouse Manager at the time. They needed someone part-time and from there I quickly escalated to doing the booking and DJing myself. Since then I've broken off and started my own DJ Company handling the booking, gear, and actual DJing on my own. It's a pretty busy day but I totally fell in love with what I do. I do feel fortunate to be one of those people that get to wake up doing what they love every day.

EPC: That is awesome. How long ago was that?

Jack: That was about five years ago.

EPC: Okay, so you finished school. Give us a condensed version of the last five years?

Jack: The last five years, I spent time working in the warehouse and then after about six months I started working in the office of the DJ Company, prepping events and making sure that everything was ready for the DJs. The DJs needed all their music and their timelines prepared for them. Then after about six months, I started working with potential couples who were looking to book a DJ for their wedding. I fell really in love with that. I really enjoyed talking with couples and with clients about special days and how they want to have the time of their lives at an event. I really found a passion for going out and meeting other vendors and working with them as well. Establishing relationships that are mutually beneficial so that both of our companies can grow.

EPC: Great. What are some of the biggest mistakes you see people making when planning their events or hiring a DJ and how do you help them avoid those things?

Jack: I think one of the biggest things that couples struggle with when they're planning events, particularly weddings are that they have a vision in mind before they've put the work in to find out how that vision is going to be executed. For instance, sometimes a client will provide a playlist or a timeline they want the DJ to follow, which is fine, but sometimes that timeline and that playlist won't work the way they fore see it working. When this happens, getting the clients to trust the DJ as an expert can sometimes be a challenge, but as a professional I always feel it's our job to communicate with them about how to make the event successful based on the many events I've seen over the course of my career.

EPC: That makes sense. How do you measure a successful event?

Jack: I primarily DJ weddings and the thing that I always look to at the end of successful events is the big hug you get from a couple at the end of the night. When the wedding couple is excited and happy that means everything went perfectly. Recently the groom gave me the big bro hug and he's like, "Thank you so much. This is awesome." My favorite bride comment is "This is the best night ever. Thank you!" To me that's the moment that I know I did a respectable job. Obviously, it's super fun to see everyone dancing and having an enjoyable time. I think that moment when the whole night is over, and you can just see that look in their eyes that this was the best of their life. That is what I measure my success to.

EPC: That's a great answer. What do you attribute your success to?

Jack: I've been very fortunate in having mentors that have been able to guide me along and help make sure that I'm doing things in the right way. I was very fortunate to be able to be an assistant DJ and learn from the best. Seeing how others do it and learning how not to do it. You learn how to pick up certain things from having a mentor, and even more importantly, you see how to keep becoming better.

I find that it's probably very difficult for someone to just learn without having someone to emulate or learn from, which is one of the reasons I love things like EPC. Because you get the chance to meet so many wonderful vendors who have been doing this for a long time and to share their experiences and their backgrounds.

EPC: Given all the fun they're having and the success you've achieved, what's your biggest challenge now?

Jack: From a DJ standpoint I'm always learning. I always like to just find the little tricks and things that other DJs do. I love to chat with other DJs about what they do and how their events go. I could talk to other DJs, or event professionals in general, for hours about their experiences. I don't know if I would say it's the biggest challenge but I think it's more just the ongoing learning process of always trying to become better than you were before and never allowing yourself to believe you've completed your journey of learning and growing.

EPC: I think that makes a lot of sense. Where do most of your clients come from?

Jack: Funny enough in this world where we have all these different marketing opportunities, I really get most of my clients just from personal relationships that I have created either with other vendors or with the clients I've worked with before. I get a lot of repeat business or people who have said, "My friend used you guys and they got married. They said I had to call you." Vendors who have said, "Hey, we've worked with you a million times and it's always been great. I'll make sure all my couples go to you guys to get married or to DJ their event."

It's just creating strong relationships with other people that has then led to being thought about at those times when a DJ is needed. Of course, things like the website has been very helpful as well. Which in a way is trying to just say an internet version of word-of-mouth. Yeah, just creating those relationships with other people, primarily with great vendors, has really been powerful for me.

EPC: Who is an ideal client for you?

Jack: For me it's just someone who is having an event and that wants to have an enjoyable time. I know that sounds very generic but one of the things that I've done is I've created a large network of DJs I know, so even if I'm not personally available, I can refer someone to the perfect fit. I try to have a wide variety of DJs with different personalities and music styles so that regardless of the type of couple they are or client they are, whether it be a corporate event or a couple, I'm going to have a good match for them. For me, I just want to have a couple or a client that's just looking to have an enjoyable time. Really the idea is that if they want to celebrate, I want to be able to celebrate with them. I think that's just a great, fun way to have an event. For me that's the ideal client.

EPC: What is the first step you would want them to take?

Jack: The   first   step,   check   out   the   website, www.jackcfarmer.com or go on social media and check out @realjackfarmer. If everything there looks like a good fit for you, give me a call or shoot me an email and we can talk. Today, it's so nice with things like Skype and FaceTime, just creating an opportunity for us to chat one-on-one about what their vision is. Then we can see if we're a good fit for each other, and if not, no worries. I'll be happy to refer them to the best DJ for their event. That's usually the first step. They go ahead, and they can give me a call or shoot me an email and we'll take it from there.

EPC: All right. Thank you so much, fascinating interview.

EPC Book Recommendation:

Last Night a DJ Saved My Life: The History of the Disc Jockey by Bill Brewster

When it rains,
look for
RAINBOWS.

CHAPTER 7
Tiffany Gillespie
To The T Events

At the Event Planners Club, we identify what makes experts like Tiffany so unique. She saves the wedding day with her emergency kit.

EPC: Tiffany Gillespie from tothetevents.biz. *To The T Events and Catering* is a premier lifestyle event design, event coordination, and catering company based in Philadelphia, Pennsylvania. With nearly a decade of experience their areas of expertise include exclusive corporate events, as well as upscale social events and elegant private affairs.

         Let's go back in time a little bit, what inspired you to be in the event planning industry?

Tiffany: I've always had a passion for wedding planning and events. I started planning events for my friends and family when I was 16 and once I went to college I started doing it more officially in the university setting helping with various organizations. I'm not honestly sure where the passion came from, I just always had a knack for organization. I was always a little bit bossy and I think that the two kinds went together. I really love beautiful things and making other people happy through the events that I create.

EPC: I'm assuming that probably being a little bit bossy comes in handy in the event planning industry. How did you get to this point in your career?

Tiffany: This was not my choice and I am always very clear as to tell people that. I went to school for criminal justice, I thought that I wanted to be a lawyer and I was just going to do event planning as kind of a side job or something that I did behind the scenes. I worked in the legal industry for about seven years and then I was fired from two jobs back to back within a one-year time span. When I was fired from the second job I just really took it as a sign that I needed to be running my business full time and to really give it my all so that's how I ended up full time in my business.

The way that I have gotten to the point that I am as far as the clientele that we had taken, the places that we traveled, the events and weddings that we have coordinated is really all been through challenging work, word of mouth, and just really promoting our business and providing amazing customer service.

EPC: Okay, that makes sense. Getting fired was probably a good thing.

Tiffany: Yeah, it was. Getting fired was probably the greatest thing that happened to me. Certainly, one of the greatest lessons. I did not feel that way when I first was fired. The first time I definitely didn't feel that way, I had never been without a job, so I literally walked around downtown Philadelphia looking for a job after they fired me because I really didn't know what I was supposed to do next. The second time I kind of had already been through this once before and I've only just took it as a sign that I needed to be running my business and everything really worked out the way that it was supposed to.

EPC: You've done events for some amazing high-profile clients, can you share with us some of your success stories?

Tiffany: Absolutely, absolutely. For the most part we really value confidentiality as far as our clients go, but we can certainly list the type of clients that we work for. We've been fortunate enough to work for one of the heirs of the Campbell's Soup Company. That was one of our first high profile clients. We have worked for publishing companies, one of which is based out of Memphis, Tennessee. We have worked for elected officials and those who were striving to be elected. One of my first experiences as far as planning events and things go, it was actually while working with the District Attorney's Office here in Philadelphia, so that was what I would consider a fairly high-profile client.

Then let's see, we currently have Black Light Magazine, we manage their events on a national level, so they are one of our higher profile clients. It's a national and international company. We've worked for pastors, churches and with various universities like Drexel, University of Pennsylvania and La Salle University.

EPC: Let me ask you this, what have been some of the biggest event planning mistakes you've seen and what did you learn from them?

Tiffany: I'm glad that you asked me that question because certainly I've made a lot of mistakes in my time and I'm big on actually sharing mistakes so other event planners can learn. I would say that one of the biggest mistakes that I think that planners make is not taking control of the event from the beginning. Now that does not mean that you take over the clients' event and make it your own, what I mean by taking control is: ensuring that you effective and clear communication from the very beginning, that you let your clients know and set the tone for how the planning process is going to go.

That provides them with some structure, it provides you with some structure, and it also helps your clients to feel more comfortable and secure in utilizing your services because they know that there is a structure and some organization behind the planning. If you don't take control from the beginning, you will have family members who try to step in and run the show, you will have venue managers who step in and try to run the show, you will have brides and grooms who kind of want to do their own thing instead of following the successful system we know works.

On the side of brides and grooms, one of the biggest downfalls that I see is that brides and grooms are not true to themselves. They allow their friends and family to come in and kind of dictate how their wedding is going to be, how the wedding planning process is going to be. That ends up leaving the bride and groom very frustrated and stressed throughout the wedding planning process and usually not having everything that they want or desire on their wedding day. Those would probably be the top two mistakes that I see.

Of course, there are a slew of mistakes that we probably all experience on the day of as far as people dropping stuff, not bringing your emergency kit, not having everything that you need in your emergency kit, not having proper staffing. Just all those various mistakes, but I would say that the two that I listed are the biggest mistakes that I see and have experienced.

EPC: That makes a lot of sense and it is very helpful. What's an emergency kit?

Tiffany: Every planner should have an emergency kit. It's like a box on wheels, so it will have safety pins, hair pins, if make up gets on material like wipes to try to remove that, anything that you can kind of think of, like a miniature sewing kit, like needle and thread is usually in there, make up removers, there are a lot of things. It's literally like a box that can handle anything happens.

EPC: If there weren't any emergencies. How do you measure a successful event?

Tiffany: To me, success is measured in smiles and I know that probably sounds so corny or cliché but that's how you know. The way that I measure a successful event, if we're doing a, let's say that it's an actual event and not a wedding, really whatever the clients goal was so for our publishing company, we know that they want to sell a certain number of books. We know that they want to have a certain number of attendees. We know that there's a certain number of products and materials that must move throughout the event or be sold at the event for them to deem it a successful event.

As far as a wedding goes, we really do measure that in smiles. It's about, if the client can say at the end of the night, "This was everything that I wanted and more", then we know that we've done our job and I think that the "and more" is important. Of course, it's going to be what they want because we've been working together for months to make it happen so it should be what they want, it's the extra that we add on as a company behind the scenes, the special touches that we put on a wedding that really blow the customers, the client rather, out of the water.

Measuring in smiles and then for events if there's like a fundraising goal or a certain number of units of a product that need to be sold, then we know that we've been successful.

EPC: That makes a lot of sense. What do you like best about your business?

Tiffany: I love my business, it's my baby. I was about to say, "I love my baby", but I wanted to explain what I was talking about first. I love my business, it's very near and dear to me. My business has literally taken on a life of its own and it helped to save my life honestly. When I lost my job, both times, I was down. I was mad. I had a lot of feelings, but having something to pour into, something to work on. Having these amazing clients who count on me and depend on me who stretch me and pull me, it certainly gave me something else to focus on and saved me from being down and depressed. I love my business. I'm super grateful for my business.

I would say that the two things actually that I love most about *To The T Events and Catering*, is the clients. I really love my clients, and I say this all the time. I constantly post it on social media. I will tell anyone I love my clients and I've been blessed to have amazing clients. I have heard some horror stories from other planners about dealing with various clienteles, but I am fortunate to be able to say that I've had amazing clients. All my clients I am still connected to, still friends with, so that's definitely one of my favorite parts, and then the flexibility that it provides me. I've spent a lot of time and I've made a lot of sacrifices staying away from friends and family and not being able to fully support everyone the way that I always wanted to so have the flexibility now is something that I definitely appreciate. I work more now than I did when I was working a 9 to 5, but I think that having that flexibility is what keeps the balance.

EPC: Absolutely. What do you attribute your success to?

Tiffany: I attribute my success to my faith. Anyone that knows me knows I love God. I am a faithful Christian, boisterous about it. Not the kind that's smacking you with a Bible or anything like that, but I just really try to live a life that is reflective of my belief and I know that all my blessings that they come from God. My faith is the center of everything that I do. It's the center of the way that I operate my business. It's the center of the way that I carry myself as a person and business owner. It's the center of the way that I interact with my clients and I think that that's why it becomes so personal because I am the planner who prays for my clients, who encourages my clients, who was there to support in and out of the planning process.

Then certainly the level of success, I pray every single day. I pray over my business, my clients, everything, so I would say certainly my faith and then the other part is demanding work. Faith without works is dead. I can pray until I'm blue in the face but if I don't get up and get the work done, nothing is going to happen. I just work very, very hard and I pray very, very hard.

EPC: Work hard, pray hard, and I'm sure there's some play in there too I hope.

Tiffany: Yes.

EPC: With all the success you've achieved, what is your biggest challenge now?

Tiffany: I would say that the biggest challenge, and this is probably always the biggest thing for most business owners, always just working to get new clients. I'm fortunate to have a lot of repeat clients but you always must be bringing in new clientele, so that part. Then figuring out how to scale your business. Our goal this year is to double what we brought in last year and we are already on track to do so, so we're just going to keep pushing forward with that goal and I think that we'll exceed it, but I know that we're going to meet it.

Figuring out how to bring in new clients and pricing, those are the 2 things that I hear a lot of business owners struggle with, I wouldn't say it's a struggle for us but that's definitely always the thing that's at the forefront.

EPC: That makes sense. What challenges do you face when you're sourcing entertainment for your client?

Tiffany: Finding people, or finding entertainment that is unique, within the client's budget, and professional, those are the top 3. Finding professional anything these days tends to be a challenge for some reason, I'm not sure why I'm so big on that. Finding, especially as far as entertainers go, because in the arts industry specifically in the music industry, there's just this horrible stereotype that musicians, singers, bands, that they're just not professional, they don't show up on time, that they really have this like negative stigma that kind of surrounds them. I've been fortunate to, through much research, have some good entertainment to be able to provide for my clients.

Certainly, finding someone who is unique within the client's budget, because clients often want things that may be out of budget. So, finding something that they want within their budget is probably the biggest challenge. Then always just making sure that not only are they going to do well, but that if you recommended them to your client that they're a good recommendation.

EPC: What drives you crazy about your business?

Tiffany: What drives me crazy? Let's see. Crazy, I don't know, that's a tough one. The most tedious thing, I think tedious is probably a better word for me; the most tedious thing about being a business owner is the business that happens behind the scenes. Being able to, like you still must manage your business financially and legally and that is something that proves to be, not really a challenge, but it's real tedious. It's the least fun part of my job, I do not like having to maintain the books, make sure that we're compliant with everything that we must be complaint with. I don't think that any business owner really loves that part of the business but it's what you must do. I would say managing the business behind the business is the parts that probably drive me the craziest.

EPC: Who is an ideal client for you?

Tiffany: I think that often if you ask this question some people may respond with a certain budget or an age or something like that. For me, ideal client is the person who understands the value of lifestyle events. We are a lifestyle company, meaning that they understand the value that is placed on having events and celebration. This is the client that's going to have a small dinner party when someone gets a promotion in their household, they're going to have a gathering when their child gets accepted to college, they're going to have the wedding, have the baby showers, the bridal showers, the birthday celebrations, anniversary celebrations, someone who really understands having a good party, having genuine fun.

Generally, that client, the type of client that will have the budget to have multiple events throughout the year, it's kind of like an automatic that they're going to be in a certain income range, they're going to live in a certain type of neighborhood, they're going to work at certain jobs. We tend to serve a more exclusive and affluent clientele and we worked hard to get to that point so I'm really grateful for that. I would say that regardless of the demographic part of it, any client that really places value on celebrations and lifestyle events is going to be our ideal client.

EPC: How do most of your clients find you?

Tiffany: Most of them find me through word of mouth. Which I think speaks a lot to what we provide for our clients, because that means that they're going down and telling other people. Most of them find us through word of mouth. Then social media, since we have really focused heavily on social media management, social media has gotten much better. We have been getting a lot of inquiries through that.

EPC: Okay, and what it the first step you would want a client to take to start a relationship with you?

Tiffany: Absolutely. They should email us at info@tothetevents.biz. They can absolutely email us at any point. They can also give us a call on our office number, they can find us on social media, and all of our contact information is on our website or on social media.

EPC Book Recommendation:

The Service Culture Handbook: A Step-by-Step Guide Getting Your Employees Obsessed with Customer Service by Jeff Toister

Being
HAPPY never
goes out of
style.

The little things, make the BIGGEST impact.

CHAPTER 8
John Goolsby
Godfather Films

At the Event Planners Club, we identify what makes experts like John so unique. He has made over 3,000 wedding videos, gotten more than 400,000 YouTube views, and delivers "time-travel" for the bride and groom.

EPC: John Goolsby of godfatherfilms.com was assigned the job of movie projector operator in the 5th grade, which is kind of prophetic. Since founding Godfather Films in 1986, they've gone on to produce more than 3000 wedding and corporate films, traveling to 30 states and 21 countries. They've got offices in California and New York and produce more than 300 video projects a year.

How did you get your start with Godfather Films?

John: I was a freshman in high school, and they had bought television equipment for the library. That was before video cameras were available to the consumer. So, I was playing with video cameras even before the public and really enjoyed it. My sophomore year they hired an algebra teacher to teach the video class, but he didn't know anything. So, I would come in a little early each day, show him a little something. Then he'd turn around and show the class. I was filming graduations, basketball games, football games, plays, school concerts, and I really, really enjoyed it.

After school I went to work in the supermarket, because that's what everybody in my family did. At age 22 I was a manager for Safeway Stores, had the most profitable store on the West Coast. Then the company went through a hostile takeover and a leveraged buyout, and it occurred to me that I may not be able to retire on that job.

So, in '86 is when I filmed my first wedding, 30 years ago this month, and I was hooked. Not only did I get a paycheck, which I need, but when I took it to the bride's house and played it for her, because she didn't own a VCR yet, she liked it so much she cried. That was a pretty good reward, too. Since then I've gone on to film more than 3000 weddings.

EPC: That is incredible, and you've done some amazing work over the years. How did you get to this point in your career?

John: Well, you must. You must evolve, or you don't survive. I landed an excellent job for a software client recently. They found me on Google to produce a film for a local company. They liked me enough that they've flown me on to 12 other states now, doing promotional films for some of their clients. I was doing one for a client in Birmingham, Alabama, a third-generation company. The guy that runs it, he says, "You know, most third generation companies in the country fail, over 90% of them." I go, "Why is that?" He says, "They don't adapt. They don't evolve." He says, "We actually require each executive who works here to work somewhere else for two years before we move them into management, and that's mostly family."

80

That really kind of made me think about my business. I remember when the economy got bad back in 2007, 2008. The video community is a relatively tight-knit community. We pretty much all know each other. I also knew that most of them were not doing well financially, that the economy had really hurt the business. But there were a handful that were doing well, and so I looked at what they were doing. One, they all had a great website. So, we redid our website. They all had a great social media presence, so we went to seminars and learned how to get better at that. They were all doing dynamite work, and some of them hadn't been in the business that long. I had, but I couldn't let my pride get the best of me; so, I've learned a lot from people who've been in business less than a year. They've come up with creative new ways of doing things, and I've just decided to learn from them, too.

EPC: That was smart. You talked about website. You talked about social media presence. You've got over 400,000 views on YouTube. How do you get so much social media attention?

John: Well, I'm active on Facebook. We're there a lot. We've got a several thousand personal and business page. I've got over 200 domain names that we promote, and that helps us get a lot of traffic.

EPC: What has been some of the biggest mistakes you've seen clients make, and how do you educate them to avoid those?

John: All right. Well, you mentioned I had how many views on YouTube?

EPC: 404,000.

John: Man, I haven't loaded anything on there in a long time. I think we've got over two million on Vimeo. That's where I put almost everything. Mistakes that clients make?

EPC: Yes, when planning their events, when planning their weddings, or when trying to choose a cinematographer or videographer to film their precious moments.

John: Well, perceptions are always off a little bit. It's education and research that educates and statistics that gives us the truth. I've worked for a lot of clients who, when they first come to see me, think that wedding video is pretty much just surveillance footage; it's just somebody setting a camera on a tripod and pointing it at them. I think maybe sometimes they don't always realize the value of it.

Let me paint a little picture. Candles are lit. Music's playing. Mothers are being seated in the front row of the church, wearing the most expensive clothing they've ever owned. The bride doesn't get to see any of that, because she hasn't made her entrance yet. The handsome groom walks to the center aisle and has some sort of reaction. He may laugh, or cry, or try not to pass out, but he's going to have a reaction that she should see someday.

Then the closest people on the planet to her are going to walk down the middle aisle: bridesmaids, groomsmen, maid of honor. There might be a flower girl and a ring bearer, really, cute, but people will have to tell her about it, because she won't see it. She won't even see her own self walk down the aisle. Usually it's a father figure that's walking her down the aisle also. He's been thinking of that moment ever since he first held her. He doesn't get to see it.

The bride and groom only get to experience 10% of their own wedding day, and we only remember 10% of what we experience. So, the day after their wedding they only have 1% in their mind of the biggest day of their life. The challenge is all memories fade, and most disappear. I'm John with Godfather Films and I sell time travel.

EPC: Wow. That is beautiful. I'm remembering my wedding right now. It's funny. I have a nine-year-old son and seven- and three-year-old daughters. My seven-year-old has watched our wedding video more than my wife has.

John: How nice. There's a lot of truth to that. I mean, potential clients will say, "Well, I'm not sure if I'll ever watch this." I kind of want to point out to them, "It's not just for you. There's going to be future generations that come along." Sometimes I'll point out to couples, "Well, like, what if we had a film of our grandparents' wedding? Not only would we get to see our grandparents, we might even get to see their grandparents, hear their words, people that we never got to meet or hear or get to know and we're related to them."

One time I had a bride that says, "Oh, we do have an 8-millimeter film of our grandparents wedding." I said, "Great. How much do you want for it? I'll buy it." She goes, "Excuse me?" I said, "I'll write you a check right

83

now. I'd love to have that footage." She says, "That's the most important thing our family owns. We would never sell it." I just looked at her. I said, "Are you getting it? That's what's going to happen to your wedding film for future generations."

EPC: That is incredible. How do you measure a successful event like that?

John: How do I measure a successful event?

EPC: Yes. How do you quantify it?

John: Gosh. I'm not exactly sure I understand, but I don't know if I could. To me, every event is successful. You've got the closest people to you on the planet all at one place, all at one time, all to see you happy. I've done weddings with four guests. I've done weddings with 2,000 guests. I've done weddings where I know they paid more for me than everything else and I've done weddings that were in the millions.

It seems like, when the bride and groom are standing there and saying their vows to each other, everything else disappears. It seems to be just as real and important to everybody no matter what's happening. A lot of times clients will ask me how I'm going to create their film. That's a hard question to answer, because the event itself will tell me how to do the film. Brides and grooms have no hidden emotions on their wedding days.

I can spend a little time with them, look at them. I can tell what they're wearing and tell how important attire is to them. I owned a wedding dress store for five years; I've got a little background on that. I can look at the location and tell how important architecture is. I can watch who they interact with and how they interact with them to know what people need to be really featured in the film. So, to me, when I go to an event like this and film it, it's like going to a movie, but being in the movie, and it's all happening in 3D around me.

We all like stories. We've been telling stories ever since we drew on cave walls. Every element of a happy story is at every wedding. You've always got the romance. You've always got the drama, the comedy, the suspense. It's all happening in real time. You'd think after 3000 weddings it might become a little predictable. I can anticipate what's going to happen, but I've never been to a boring wedding.

EPC: That is so true. What do you attribute your success to?

John: I remember reading a Forbes magazine article where they had interviewed leading CEOs and they had asked them the same question. The overwhelming answer was 'persistence.' I've done quite a few seminars and I like to portray stories, or share stories, about people who just had incredible odds. They couldn't make it, and they did. So, I think it's just the number one thing is just not giving up.

As far as doing weddings, I think it's buying into what marriage is. I tell my kids that the goal in life is to be old and in love, and that all starts with the commitment a couple makes on their wedding day. I had a client in my office one time and I was talking about the importance of wedding video, and our love stories, and how we interview couples about how they met and share that story. She starts grinning at me, like non-stop, and I go, "Is it funny?" She says, "Well, I'm a clinical psychologist." We both just stopped and looked at each other. Here I'm telling her about relationships. She said, "It's absolutely true, what you're saying."

It seems like a lot of times when people get married, boom, they check that off their list and then they go on to other things that are important in their life. Then they start neglecting and taking advantage of the most important things to them. Every wedding I've ever filmed, every time I've seen the groom look down the aisle at his bride walking towards him, there's this realization in his eyes about how lucky he really is. Every time I've heard a bride say her wedding vows to her husband, I can hear her growing more in love by the emotion in her voice. I don't want them to ever forget that. I want to provide them a vehicle that allows them to go back to that time anytime they want to or anytime the relationship needs them to.

I've always believed when you fall in love you're always in love, just sometimes you need a little help in getting back to that spot. When I think of all the services that are available to a wedding, I can't think of anything that can transport a couple back to that time better than a wedding film, at least if it's a good one.

EPC: Absolutely. Who is an ideal client for you?

John: I had a bride call me yesterday. It's happened a few times. They start off the conversation by telling me that video isn't important to them, but everybody keeps telling them that they're going to regret it if they

86

don't. That's not good for my ego. It's really good when somebody calls, "Oh, I've seen your work. You're amazing. I want to hire you. Oh, you're not available on my date. Okay, I'll change my date," which has happened.

The ideal client, I guess, is the one who watches the film later. Well, I've got two notes sitting on my desk right now from today's mail, telling me how much they love their wedding film; how little they remember; how this has brought back so many good memories to them and how they're going to have them for the rest of their life now. I guess that would be my ideal client who really loves their wedding film and then becomes my advertising by telling others.

EPC: How does your process work from initial consultation to final delivery?

John: Well, we're making a custom film. When somebody makes a film for the masses that's going to play at the theatre, that film must appeal to millions. When I'm making a film, it only has to appeal to the people sitting in the room in front of me, and it could be a very small group. So, the more I get to know about them, visit with them, learn what's important to them, that helps me make a better film.

We'll have an initial consultation. We'll talk; they'll share what's important to them. Then we'll come out and we'll film everything that happens that day. We'll have several cameramen. We'll have several cameras. We'll have a drone in the air. We'll have gimbals, which give you stabilized moving shots. We film all of that without interacting with people. It's not unusual for us to go an entire day without speaking to anybody there. We really want it to look like a film. In the film Brad Pitt doesn't wave at the camera and say, "Hi, mom," so that's not what we're looking for.

We'll film it all and then we'll bring it back to our studio. I have seven full-time employees. We're doing about 300 projects a year. One of my employees, my IT guy, is responsible for taking all the cards and archiving them; so, they're backed up to a Drobo, which is a redundant storage thing, to make sure they're safeguarded. Then we copy them again to another hard drive that one of my editors will be working on.

Then each project is assigned to an editor, and the editor will create the film. We will create several films. We have a unique ability right now to deliver everything in HD, which is six times the resolution of a DVD. So, we have custom hard drives, where we'll put a highlight film on there, which is a 6-10-minute film that catches everything that happened that day in a highlight manner. People love that. They put that on their Facebook; they put it on their phone. When they go on their break at work, instead of looking at a couple of still shots, they're showing their music video to their family and friends.

Then we'll put full-length versions of the ceremony, with the speeches, the special dances, all those things. They get a full-length edit of that. So, now they're getting four or five movies. Then we'll create social media files that load a little faster and then we'll put all the raw footage on that hard drive. So, everything we film that day, they get to watch. If I was a bride or groom, I'd want to see everything that happened at some point. I may not watch it every day, but I'd definitely want to have it.

Then we put on the hard drive all the film assets. Those would-be music, graphics, title, even the edit decision list; so, in theory, if they want to make some changes to this film years down the road, we should be able to plug the hard drive into the software and have it all open again. I don't know anybody else who makes the deliverables the way we do. I really want my clients to be happy, and I think one of the mindsets that I want to have is, "What would I want to have?" I'd want to have it all, so that's what we give our clients.

EPC: That is an excellent answer and a beautiful process. Fascinating interview, incredible story. Anything else you want to share that I didn't think to ask you?

John: Well, who's our audience? Is it other people in the industry?

EPC: Yes, other people in the event planning, wedding planning, industry. Yeah.

John: Well, I've got to tell you that sometimes-wedding professionals, especially when we have our artist mentality working for us, we're creative, unique. We use our mind to create what we do. All that's true, but things have changed so much in the event industry in the last century, the last decade, the last year, sometimes in the last month, and it's not always easy to stay up-to-date with that; but, by participating with professional trade associations or if there's something new happening, you're going to be the first to know it. So, when your client mentions it, you're all over it.

I remember going to a trade association meeting, and the president gets up and says, "I want you to know I don't recommend people in this room." There's a quiet in the room, like, "Darn. That's why I'm here. I want to get referred." She says, "I refer friends in this room." There's something about the social setting that trade associations provide wedding professionals, where you can sit down and talk, and visit, and have a meal with somebody else in the industry. Our company is on 50 different vendor lists for hotels and country clubs; but, if you call those hotels and country clubs and try and set up a meeting with a decision maker and all that, you may never get through the door. By participating in a trade association, you could be having lunch and dinner with these people every month.

So, I think it's one of the best investments you can make, is to get involved with a trade association and get to know people. You'll learn a lot, you'll build your business, and you'll develop some great friendships.

EPC: All right. Thank you very much. Fascinating interview. I've got tons of notes. I'm sure our readers will too. We greatly appreciate your time. We've been here with John from Godfather Films. Thank you so much.

EPC Book Recommendation:

The Traveler's Gift by Andy Andrews

"A positive MINDSET sees speed bumps, not obstacle."

CHAPTER 9
Jenny Hill
JC Room Blocks

At the Event Planners Club, we identify what makes experts like Jenny so unique. She creates a magical experience for wedding guests by extending the party into the hotel block.

EPC: Jenny Hill, the co-owner of JC Room Blocks at JCRoomBlocks.com is sharing her secrets. What inspired you to be in the event planning industry?

Jenny: I've always had a love of weddings. Ever since I was a little kid, I loved dreaming about what my wedding would be like. I love going to weddings. I started just looking in the event planning realm when I went to work for a meeting and convention planning company. There I would help set up blocks of sleeping rooms for large events and conventions and in doing that I just had a lot of friends and family members who were getting married and just had no idea how to set up room blocks for themselves. My business partner Catherine Keffer and I had the idea to start setting up blocks of rooms for weddings and extraordinary events specifically. That's how we broke into this business.

EPC: How did you get from there to this point in your career?

Jenny: Oh my Gosh. It took a lot. As I mentioned, we were working in the meeting and convention planning realm. When we decided to start our business, we had to become a full-fledged travel agency. You must jump through a lot of hoops to do that. We did all the necessary things to become a certified travel agency. I worked a second job. I waited tables for two years to just make it happen. We started picking up speed and our clients would tell other clients. We started being featured online, on different films like Wedding Wire and the Knot and lots of online places. We just exploded over the last few years.

It's just taken a lot of support from our clients and a lot of love from our family and friends, but we're doing it. We're making it happen.

EPC: That is incredible.

Jenny: Thank you.

EPC: What are some of your biggest mistakes you see people make when planning weddings and how do you help them avoid those mistakes?

Jenny: I think a lot of people tend to think that not setting up a room block is the way to go. We find time and time again that brides and grooms and bridal couples get burned that way. Depending on when they're getting married and the time of year, there could be several competing events going on in where they're getting married, in the location, and that could really discourage, and it could really be very hurtful to people trying to get rooms in that area. Like if there's a city-wide convention happening and then all rooms are overbooked, or they can't get a room. Having a block of really guarantees that those rooms are going to be available to their guests.

Plus, if you go through a company like mine and that's being a certified travel agency, we're able to get the lowest possible rates that aren't offered to the public. I think when bridal couples want to just do this on their own or they decide not to set up a block, sometimes down the road that can lead to a lot of issues and problems for their guests with having to pay crazy high rates or not being able to find rooms at all.

EPC: That makes sense. How do you measure a successful event?

Jenny: I think we really tailor fit what we do to our clients, so we have some clients that are looking for just the most economical options for their guests and we do all we can to fit their needs and try to find what they're looking for in their hotels and accommodations. Then we have other clients who really want that luxury full-service feel and they want to book the most luxurious hotels around.

I think the way that we measure what's a successful event, is it's just really tailored to the client because we work with so many different budgets and so many different visions of what our clients are looking for.

EPC: Absolutely. What do you like best about what you do?

Jenny: I love being a part of people's biggest days of their lives. Although, it is a smaller part, just being able to put their vision together and work closely with them and go on this journey with them. It's so exciting. It's so thrilling and rewarding. When we can just help our clients find the best possible accommodations, when we can get them their free bridal suite or get the hotel the biggest chocolate-covered strawberries or champagne to them the night of their wedding. It's so rewarding.

EPC: Absolutely. What do you attribute your success to?

Jenny: I think that for Catherine and me, we're very small company so we work on all our accounts together. I think really having that personalized touch and the personalized service that we can offer really sets up apart from our competitors. It's not like you're going to fill out an online submission form and you're going to be just exchanging emails back and forth. We really hold our clients' hands from beginning to end. We act as their advocates. We get them and try to get them whatever they're looking for at the hotel of their choice. I think really getting down and dirty and working directly with the client really gives them access to the owners of the company and really sets us apart from other competitors out there.

EPC: Absolutely. With all the success you've achieved, what is your biggest challenge now?

Jenny: I think now it's just about growing the business that we have and how to control the growth. Like I mentioned before, we are a relatively smaller company. It's just myself and my business partner, Catherine. Incredibly, we do about 300 weddings a year, but that number is growing, which is fantastic.

We are so happy that that's happening, but how do we continue to offer the personalized customer service that we're known for, but then expand and grow? How do we take people on and train them to care as much as we do and being able to provide that same level of service at a larger scale?

EPC: That makes a lot of sense. You're doing 300 weddings a year? That's an incredible number. Where do most of your clients come from?

Jenny: Yeah. They come from all over. We work nationwide and into Canada and the Caribbean and Mexico. People find us online and then since we've just done so many weddings thus far, people just refer us to friends and family members. We do one person's wedding and then they tell their work colleague and then they tell their sister and then they tell their cousin and then suddenly, we have five new accounts that came from one client. I'm sure that's per the usual in this industry. Referrals are everything.

Aside from that, we are lucky to have our clients just singing our praises online so there are a lot of different forums where they write full articles about us or just reviews that people can find on sites like the Wedding Wire, The Knot, even Yelp. People find us that way and I think that they're attracted to want to work with us because we do offer so much. Aside from setting up their room blocks, we can also help with getting shuttle service to and from their venue. We can help set up food and beverage functions like if they want to have a welcome reception or a rehearsal or even a close-knit bridal brunch at the hotel. We can really help to facilitate those as well.

I think it's like even if they don't have a planner, they've got somebody in their corner that can advocate for them and help with all things hotel.

EPC: That is incredible. You talked about managing the growth. How do you manage the financial aspects of your business?

Jenny: Well, that part of it has been a huge learning curve. We've really had to make it up as we go, but quite recently, we've been using QuickBooks and we've hired an accountant to help us, just because everything's happening so quickly, which is great and we're very, very lucky, but it's just like, we didn't go to school for business. I have a background in theater and my business partner, Catherine, has a background in art. The business side of everything is a little challenging for us so we did need that support and hiring key people like having an accountant, like having QuickBooks that can really help us to manage all the finances have been just godsends to us. We like to focus on working directly with the clients and doing the work that helps us quite a bit. Thank goodness for accountants and QuickBooks.

EPC: You piqued my interest. My original undergraduate degree is in acting. Tell me about your theater background.

Jenny: Musical theater is my thing. I've done theater for my entire life. I love, love, love being on stage. My undergrad is theater as well. Have done a lot of different shows. I always will have a love for it, but making it a career, you must sacrifice so much. I want a family. I want to be able to travel and to have a good life and if you work through acting as a career, you really must sacrifice so much. I'm sure you know that too, Seth, having that as a background as well. I love theater. I want to be involved in it in some way and even if that's working behind the scenes. I was part of a theater company here in LA for many years. I would like to get back into theater at a community level. You know, just doing musicals and stuff here. You can't get that feeling from anything else.

EPC: Awesome. For those folks who are looking to have the hotel room block taken care of for them in the most efficient manner, we should send them to JCRoomBlocks.com, is that correct?

Jenny: That is correct. Check us out on our website and we would love, love, love to help anybody out there looking for a room block for their event. Just so everybody knows too, although we do specialize in weddings, we have worked in other realms. We can certainly do room blocks for corporate events or other social events like bachelor/bachelorette parties, family reunions. Really, we run the gamut there. If there are planners out there listening and they have other events that aren't necessarily weddings, if it's more than ten rooms that you're looking for per night, we can certainly help. Another note too, for our planner partners we waive our fee so it's a completely free service to planners. For just brides and grooms that are going to paying, we just charge a one-time fee of $30 and that is it. You get everything that we offer for just a one-time fee of $30.

EPC: That is incredible. Fascinating interview. I am fascinated. I'm sure our readers will be too. We've

2

been talking to Jenny Hill, the co-owner of JCRoomBlocks.com. Jenny, thank you so much for joining us today.

Jenny: It has been my pleasure. Thank you, EPC.

EPC Book Recommendation:

The Best Exotic Marigold Hotel: A Novel
by Deborah Moggach

YOU
create the
experience!

CHAPTER 10
Rev. Clint Hufft
Wedding Officiant

At the Event Planners Club, we identify what makes experts like Clint so unique. His gift to the bride and groom is a heartfelt ceremony and $100 in honor of the referring vendor.

EPC: Reverend Clint Hufft is sharing his secrets to success.

Clint: It is my pleasure. Thank you.

EPC: You offer wedding ceremony podcasts in addition to some other services. Why don't we go back in time a little bit? Let's go back to when you first got the calling to be a reverend, and then we'll go from there.

Clint: Twenty years ago, is when I got ordained, non-denominational. I don't have a set ceremony. I let every couple kind of build their own ceremony. As most metropolitan areas, we get a ton of people that fall in love but they come from different backgrounds, so finding a way for them to express not only what they feel for each other, but why they're making this big commitment in a way that honors who they are as individuals and perhaps sometimes their families, but it's the individual that they fell in love with and the individual that they're offering to this person that they love, that they're going to make this big commitment of getting married and I always tell every bride, "You got to say exactly what you want to say. You got to hear exactly what you want to hear," and that discovery process is awesome.

That's kind of the way it works. I don't have a brick and mortar. I'm service oriented and do everything I can to help people.

EPC: How did you get to this point in your career?

Clint: It's interesting. Some of it is challenging work. You try to figure out how I can make myself available for people to find me so that I can help as much as possible. My business model is referral based, that's my entire business model. I think of the couple as being the people that I'm helping provide brilliant memories of this incredible day, but I'm very clear on who my actual client is. In my opinion, because I'm a referral based business, my client is the person that sent the couple to me, because it's the referral base that is repeat business, whereas the couple, once they get married, typically they may call me for a baby or some other occasion in their family, but often, once they get married, they don't need me anymore.

It's the person that puts me on their referral list, preferred vendors list, that I think is the most valuable, and I do everything that I possibly can to make sure that I make their life better and they enjoy working with me.

EPC: That makes a lot of sense. What are some of the mistakes that couples are making when planning their wedding and talking to you that you see?

Clint: I think it's typical human behavior, which is we tend to be shortsighted. I'm not sure why that is, why that's in the human DNA, but it's very easy for all of us to get caught up in the immediacy, what we perceive as being important, which often is what people tell us is important. The mistakes that couples make are thinking more in terms of what other people will think of their wedding as opposed to the experience that they want to have with each other. That can go across the entire wedding experience in terms of why they pick a venue or whom they invite.

For me, because I'm connected to everything that has to do with the wedding ceremony, a bride or a couple that says to me that in their opinion the ceremony is the most important part of the day, I tell them they immediately shoot up my list of brides towards the top, because yes, I'm biased, it is my world and the ceremony is what I focus on and where I provide my talents and skills, but what they're really saying to me is this is not just a party. This really is a momentous milestone in our lives.

What I've said often to my friends or anybody that I meet, and they just got engaged, I say, "Do yourself a favor. Think of what you want to say when you exchange your vows. Think of what you want to say to this person. If you know in your heart of hearts, how you want to express the love and commitment that you're making, and you're rock solid with who you are as individuals and who you are as a couple, then believe it or not, all the other decisions that you make for your wedding day will become much easier. This is because you're going to have a central core that everything will kind of filter through." When couples start from the outside in as opposed to the inside out, I think that's the mistake they make.

EPC: That's great advice. How do you measure a successful wedding?

Clint: It's so subjective; everybody has his or her own criteria. There's always something that doesn't go the way we thought it should or would, but you know how it is when you talk to a wedding professional about how was your weekend? It was great. Well, this didn't go the way I thought it would and that vendor kind of let me down, but you know what? The bride was happy, so we're all good. I know that's broad strokes but to me it depends on the participant.

I always believe that all that matters is what happens between the couple getting married, the connection between the couple getting married. To me, if they look across from each other and they see in that other person's eyes that that person is exactly where they want to be and they're doing exactly what they want to do, and they still want to get married and have kids. We're amazed our wives want to hang around with us, much less marry us. If they see that look in the eye, to me, from my perspective, that's a successful wedding.

Everybody else has his or her own criteria. Florists need to get to the venue and they need to be able to set up, and disc jockeys need to know what to play and how do I load in. Wedding coordinators need a million answers for a million things so that they can provide the best service, so everybody will have a different idea of what the criteria for a successful wedding is.

EPC: Very true. What do you like best about what you do?

Clint: Oh my gosh! I have the best seat in the house for this amazing moment that happens with this couple. I like people. I'm more of an introvert, but I really do like people. Hearing a couple share their story about how they met and what it is they like in each other, I pick up a lot of that through their non-verbal cues, the way they interact, how they speak, what they say about each other, and everything that surrounds them when they create their wedding ceremony. They're going to go through something that they've never gone through before typically, if they're getting married for the first time.

Even some people that got married before and didn't feel connected to the process, when they come to me and they realize that they're going to discover their ceremony, it's because I give them a ton of resources. This way there is will be no conversations sparked between the two people that probably have never come up before, and who knows, they may never come up again. It's that level of discovery about each other, I like this reading or I like this ritual because it reminds me of this or it makes me feel like this, and you know as well as I do that no matter how long you're married, you're continually discovering things about your spouse. But, what they discover about each other and for each other as they get ready for their wedding ceremony and then the brilliance of the moment when times seems to stop, I tell people that the laws of time and physics don't work the same on your wedding day.

You're going to be involved with a moment and it's

only going to happen on your wedding day, and while you're in the middle of it it'll feel like it's lasting forever, but then you'll blink your eyes and you're waving goodbye to everybody. My favorite part is when time slows down and when they are caught up in the rapture of getting married and everything that kind of built to that moment, and I get to guide them. I get to guide them from before, as they walk the processional, as they come in to me, and then when they leave they're different. They've crossed over a threshold, and it is awesome.

EPC: That is beautiful. What do you attribute your success to?

Clint: I'm very lucky. Part of it is being in the right place at the right time, but also everything in my life has trained me for this job, and it is the best job I've ever had in my life. You know how the number one phobia in America is public speaking? I'm the opposite. I don't know what it is, but that's just how I'm built. When I was a kid, if there was a camera I would want to be in front of it. When I was eleven, the principal of my high school asked me to be the master of ceremonies for the school talent show and I've found my calling, and I've been in front of people ever since.

That's a big part of being an officiant, is that public speaking, but I also tell people it's the perfect storm. My entire life has been diverse. I've done a ton of things in the entertainment industry, in front of the camera, behind the camera and everything, stage, commercials, television, movies, but understanding that a wedding ceremony is also theater, there's something happening in front of a group of people, and the logistics of it are important, because I don't want anything to break the connection between the two people.

While my background is a ton of live theater and production, so I understand the role that everybody plays, I'm not the boss, but anything I can do to make sure that nothing slips through the cracks, that what we need is there and everybody who is going to participate knows what we want them to do and when we want them to do it, then from that standpoint I'm really lucky that I have the experience to be able to walk into that environment and immediately say we need to move that, or we need to talk to that person and say: "I have no rules. Yes, I'm the officiant, and when they get in front of me it's kind of my ballgame, but I have no rules. Be brilliant. Get the shots you need. That's what they're going to have for the rest of their lives, but do you know what's about to happen?"

When I ask that question, one hundred percent of the time, this goes for photographers and videographers, they'll look at me and say, "Now, what?" It's not just a cookie cutter experience. Every couple has kind of like a unique way. They may or may not want to involve their parents. They may want to go to a table to pour some wine, or somebody may walk up to do a reading, or they may ask for their parents' blessings and those parents will rise. Anyway, whatever it is, I know the people with cameras want to get that shot, and usually it's just one take, although I tell every bride if we get to the end of the ceremony and you want to do it again, I'm going to say, "Let's do it again." That hasn't happened in twenty years.

The point is that I want everybody to be able to put their best foot forward from their perspective, and one of the things that I've done in my life is I was a video editor for weddings and Bar Mitzvahs back in the day when everything was all on VHS tape, so I understand that you have one shot to get it right, and if I can say, "Here's what's about to happen and it's going to happen over there," and if I can also say, "I have no rules. Get your shot." If I feel them trying to shoot over my shoulder, I'll take that little three inches move to the other side to open that up so they have a better frame, because it all serves the same thing, which is how can we make these people blissfully happy?

EPC: That is incredible. Where do most of your weddings come from?

Clint: Through referrals primarily. I would say seventy percent comes from referrals. I have a web presence, and so some people will come directly to me from that, but most of it comes from wedding professionals sharing my name and suggesting that they give me a call, and I don't take that lightly. That's a huge blessing. My business model is anybody that comes to me from a referral, I immediately take a hundred dollars off of my fee to give back to the couple, and I tell the couple, "The reason you're getting this discount is because of that person's referral, because I hold that person in high esteem and they could refer anybody, but for some reason they gave you my name and number, and that is a huge compliment and I don't take that lightly, so let me pay back to you because of them."

EPC: That makes a lot of sense. What is the first step you would want that couple to take to start the process of engaging with you?

Clint: I think it's important that they understand kind of my rhythm, so any couple that contacts me, and I mean the initial contact, I offer a huge document. I call it my wedding ceremony choices. It contains anything that anybody has ever brought me that they wanted in their wedding ceremony. After twenty years it's huge. It's a behemoth. I tell people, "This thing is ridiculously too big." It's eighty pages long, but I try to make it as user friendly as possible. It's organized as one huge ceremony. You're not going to go back and forth between ceremony number one and ceremony number two. That never made any sense to me.

I give them the document and I tell them, "You don't have to do anything with this. I just want you to know what all of your options are, that's the biggest thing." Then if they want to get involved with that, because every now and then a couple will say, "I don't want to bother with that. I just want somebody to show up and get us married," I can do that, but often when I let them know that they have an opportunity, a once-in-a-lifetime opportunity to find the exact words that will share their heart's desires with this person that they love, ninety-nine percent of the couples really jump at the opportunity, and then I guide them through that.

The only thing that they really must do is just do a little bit of homework. If we head down the homestretch there are some couples that just don't have time to do whatever a vendor needs them to do, then I take it upon myself to create a ceremony and send it to them and say, "This is what I think, based on our conversations and what you've sent me so far, I think this is what you want to experience in your wedding ceremony. Please feel free to change anything, but this is where I think we're going to go," if they haven't had time to actually work with me and whittle down the document and find their ceremony.

EPC: That makes a lot of sense. What else do you want people to know about what you're doing that I didn't think to ask you?

Clint: The ceremony podcast, the wedding ceremony podcast. My partner is JP Reynolds, and JPRweddings.com. We've been doing it on coming up on two years. It'll be two years in February. We just recorded our eighty-sixth episode. We do it once a week. We talk for about twenty-five minutes and we tell stories of what we've experienced as officiants. We didn't know how long the podcast was going to last. We did it as just a let's see, I think we have stories to tell, and let's see how long this goes, but here we are two years later and it's amazing. We've never run out of stuff to talk about. Every weekend we seem to experience something that we've never experienced before.

We laugh a lot. JP is a very funny guy. We both have been in the business for over twenty years, and every now and then we'll have a guest. That's the biggest thing, is the wedding ceremony podcast. JP is an accomplished author and we tell you about his books and things, but the best part is how lucky we feel that we get to do what we do and help the people on their biggest day.

EPC: All right. I couldn't have expressed it any better myself, Reverend Clint, for taking the time to share with us your beautiful and inspiring message.

Clint: It's my pleasure. Thank you.

EPC Book Recommendation:

ROOM FULL OF REFERRALS® ..."*and how to network for them!*" by Dr. Tony Alessandra

Never be afraid to start over.

CHAPTER 11
Marie Kubin
Rent My Wedding

At the Event Planners Club, we identify what makes experts like Marie so unique. She created Netflix for weddings, drop shipped to your door.

EPC: Marie Kubin from rentmywedding.com went from law school to event planning.

Marie: Rent My Wedding is a nationwide online event rental company. We provide décor rentals including wedding lighting, linens, canopies, backdrops, photo booths, and more. The way it works is that clients order online, rentals are shipped to their door, and afterwards clients put everything back in the same box for return. Shipping is free both ways nationwide.

The goal of Rent My Wedding is to make wedding décor easy and affordable. There are options for any budget! What sets us apart is not only our low pricing, but also our reputation for excellence. We are proud to have more 5-star reviews than any other company in the U.S. wedding industry. This track record has been established by creating a rental system that is easy, affordable, and flawless. We guarantee that every single rental order arrives on time and in perfect working condition. And we work hard to make sure we live up to that promise for every single client. I started the company while I was a bride planning my own wedding, so I know how important it is that everything is absolutely perfect for the big day.

About five years ago, I was planning my own wedding to be held in my hometown in Wisconsin while going to law school in Maryland. As I went through the process I had a few challenges, and that's what inspired me to create new rental options for the wedding industry.

The first thing I found was how difficult it was coordinating with long distance vendors. Most of them wanted to meet in person to talk about pricing and details, which was hard for me being out of state. I really wished I could just get all the info online! The other thing I found is that things like wedding lighting, draping, and photo booths were way out of my budget. These two challenges motivated me to find a way to make wedding décor easier, and to make it possible on any budget.

That's where I really got inspired. I purchased my own lighting equipment and décor, and then posted classified ads online to try to rent it out to other brides who were also trying to save money. That kind of snowballed the whole thing. After I recouped my investment, people were still interested. That's how the website started. I called it Rent My Wedding.

EPC: That is incredible that you figured out a way to overcome issues and then started helping other brides do the same.

Marie: Absolutely, it's been an amazing experience figuring out how to plan my wedding on a budget, and then helping other couples do the same.

EPC: How distinct are the types of things are you renting for weddings?

Marie: We do everything. We offer diverse types of lighting, including uplighting, gobo's, cake spotlights, centerpiece spotlights, water effect lighting, starry night lighting, moving dance floor lights, and more. We also rent linens, backdrops, canopies, pipe and drape, and photo booths.

EPC: How does that business work? Do you physically keep all of this in inventory and ship or do you have vendors around the country? How does that process work?

Marie: Yes we own all the inventory and everything ships directly from our warehouse. The rental process is really easy. People just order online. We ship it right to their door and then afterwards they put it back in the same box and ship it back to us.

EPC: Wow, so kind of like Netflix for weddings.

Marie: Exactly.

EPC: Okay, and what are some of the challenges that your brides are running into that you are helping with? Are there any logistical issues? How does that work?

Marie: Of course the number one challenge is always budget. People are always looking for ways to save money, so that's a challenge that we try to help them with. Our specialty is rental products that normally would be a big-ticket item, but we offer it for a budget price. Part of the reason why we are able to cut costs significantly is with do-it-yourself setup.

EPC: Forgive the ignorance, does that come with instructions? I've tried to assemble furniture, I can't even imagine wedding stuff, so how does that work?

Marie: Yes, the rentals come with instructions, and everything is super easy for anyone to set up. We've had everyone from kids to grandparents setting up these products for events. Believe me, anyone can do it! We've specially developed our products so that they are user-friendly, and we also provide instructions that are very easy to follow. There are printed instructions sent along in the rental package, as well as an online app and instructional videos. We also have a 24/7 helpline, so we're always just a phone call away!

EPC: 24/7 is incredible, so almost like a doctor you've got people on call. Because a lot of times, weddings and receptions and parties take place at night, so if I've got an issue at 9:30 pm I can reach somebody.

Marie: Yes, exactly and our afterhours team is amazing. They know every product inside and out so no matter what your question, they can always answer it right there on the spot. It just takes a matter of minutes to set up any of our rental products.

EPC: That is incredible. How are you getting the word out

about your service?

Marie: We primarily get the word out online. Google search is how most people find us, as well as word of mouth referrals from other people who have used us.

EPC: Okay, what do you like best about your business?

Marie: I would say what I like best is our mission that we're helping people save money, so we really feel good about what we're doing here. I also love the innovation aspect. I enjoy tackling technical or complex products like lighting or photo booths, and finding a way to make them portable and easy for anyone to set up. Our mission along with the product innovation is what I really love the most about working with Rent My Wedding.

EPC: What is your biggest challenge now?

Marie: My biggest challenge is educating the planners and the brides and grooms so that they understand that they *can* set up these technical décor items themselves. Most people assume you need to bring in a full-service professional for every aspect of their décor. While there is certainly a time and a place for full-service vendors, there _are_ other options. I think most don't necessarily realize there are other options out there, or that they can create the wedding of their dreams by looking for DIY options for their rentals. So I would say the biggest challenge right now is education and awareness.

EPC: Obviously, you have expanded your inventory

beyond the original things you needed for your own wedding. How do you evaluate vendors when choosing to work with them?

Marie: We do a lot of product testing. We test out products in-house, as well as doing testing with event professionals. We go through an extensive vetting process before finalizing a supplier.

EPC: That makes sense. So you've got constant turnover, inventory going out and coming back. How do you manage the logistics?

Marie: We have a custom-built system that allows us to manage the logistics. Using the system, we can track every detail of the rental process, manage inventory, and monitor packages in transit. This means that every transaction is seamless, and inventory is always accurate. Then on the other side of it our team is really dedicated to making sure that everything is perfect. We have a team devoted to monitoring all systems and ensuring everything goes smoothly for every order. We monitor every single package while in transit with FedEx. On the shipping side, our warehouse team tests every single item before shipping to make sure it is in perfect working condition. We also have every single order inspected twice before shipping. The combination of automated systems and physical checkpoints allows us to guarantee that every single rental is flawless.

EPC: How do you manage the financial aspects of your business?

Marie: During law school I studied tax and finance so I

handle most of this myself.

EPC: You touched on something. You were going to law school for tax and finance and then have turned into this. How do you feel about that?

Marie: I could not be happier. I loved studying the law and I did finish the degree and passed the bar (I'm a member of the Florida Bar). But, it was amazing to see this opportunity arise out of my wedding planning. I've always loved business and entrepreneurship. This passion for business along with my legal training was the perfect combination. I'm able to have this creative outlet for innovation while at the same time having a good foundation for how to start and run a company. It was really helpful to have the legal background in the startup phase for things like entity formation, getting a trademark, rental contracts, website copyrights, etc. It was great that I could rely on all these areas that I learned in law school.

EPC: Awesome. What drives you crazy about your business?

Marie: I would say that what drives me crazy about my business is...myself! I'm a perfectionist, so I spend a lot of time over-analyzing everything. There have definitely been many sleepless nights analyzing everything about the business and thinking about ways to perfect the system! The good news is that now we've gotten to a really great place where literally every aspect of the rental process has been vetted and analyzed. There is a procedure and backup plan in place for just about anything and everything that could happen, from ordering to FedEx shipping to returns.

EPC: I would imagine FedEx and shipping insurance is probably a significant expense for your business because, it's not like you're shipping envelopes.

Marie: Right, exactly that is one big area for us. The way it works is that clients receive free shipping both ways on all rentals, anywhere in the continental U.S. We guarantee that all items will arrive on time and in perfect working condition.

EPC: Wow, what a great guarantee. Who is an ideal client for you?

Marie: For us the ideal client is really anyone who wants to save money! We work with couples, wedding professionals, and Fortune 500 companies. Our client base is really just anyone looking for ways to create a "Wow" factor for their event while still sticking with a budget.

EPC: What is the first step you would want them to take to start a relationship with you?

Marie: The first step would be to visit our website, which is RentMyWedding.com. From there, you can either order online, or order by phone at 1-800-465-8020. It's as simple as that!

EPC: Okay, anything you want to share that I didn't think to ask you?

Marie: One thing I would love to share is how event

planners can really expand beyond planning and offer wedding rental packages to their clients. This includes lighting, linens, photo booths, and backdrops. Planners can book a package for a client, rent the items from us, and then set up the items for the client's event. Afterwards, the planner just puts everything back in the same box for return. This is a great way for a wedding planner to add value to clients! And clients love this because they don't have to worry about multiple contracts with multiple vendors. It's really a win-win!

EPC: Okay great advice, great interview, and awesome resource. We greatly appreciate your insights Marie, at rentmywedding.com.

EPC Book Recommendation:

Dropshipping: Complete Guide to Start Your Six-Figure Dropshipping Business NOW! How to Find Profitable Niches and Make Passive Income with Shopify, Amazon FBA, Ebay, Retail Arbitrage
by Andrew Daniels

CHAPTER 12
Katrina McGregor
Tartan Talent

At the Event Planners Club, we identify what makes experts like Katrina so unique. She is inside the red-carpet ropes working with celebrities for charities.

EPC: Welcome Katrina McGregor of TartanTalent.com. Tell us a bit about your life before you became an event planner, booking and production guru.

Katrina: I grew up in Fresno, California. Humble roots. My dad was a dentist and my mom was a homemaker.

EPC: How'd you get started in business?

Katrina: I worked for years for doctors and surgeons in my 20s and early 30s, and everybody thinks they're so difficult to work with but that wasn't my experience. Probably because my father was a dentist. I was used to personalities that needed attention to detail and I found it easy to meet their needs. This led to an easy transition to celebrity clients later.

When I was working for doctors and surgeons I got an opportunity to work for a major headliner as a personal assistant for four years, and toward the end of the four years I was working in production for him. I'll write a book when he dies so everybody knows him. There's hints on my website.

I just got tired of doing the same show every night so started working for a company when I was in San Jose that worked for fundraisers like I do now. But I found out he was very, very untrustworthy. He got a lot of people fired. I thought I could do such a better job at this and make people happy and be honest, so I started my company soon after that. I do fundraising and special event now.

EPC: Congratulations that sounds like an incredible journey. What is the biggest challenge you've had to overcome, and more importantly what did you learn from it?

Katrina: I think the biggest challenge is when the internet came to be. People started thinking they could do this themselves, and they still kind of do. That's probably the biggest challenge. Anyone in my business thinks it can happen. What it is, is there's an enormous difference when someone who knows how to put on a concert or a speaking event, and knows how to contract and negotiate on the organizations behalf, knows all the ins and outs from the offer to putting them back on the plane can do it with their eyes closed. I think it's a dramatic difference than somebody who's struggling with every snag.

EPC: That makes a lot of sense. You worked with some incredible celebrities over your career. How did you get to build those relationships?

Katrina: Here's how a typical job goes for me. Somebody wants, say Tony Bennett, for their fundraiser this year. I make an offer, it gets accepted, hopefully and usually. If not that's the negotiation thing, and we start producing the show.

I get to know everyone in Tony Bennett's camp over the at least four months we'll have to work on this. You get to know people and that's your friend from then on because you worked on a show together. Then you tend to work on more shows together because they know you when you put an offer in.

An example of many relationships I made at once was booking United Negro College Fund one year. I booked Stevie Wonder, Ashford and Simpson, Freddy Jackson, The Commodores, Brian McKnight. I booked huge acts, and all at once I knew all those entourages and staff members. When I showed up for the taping it was like old home week and we're all friends, because they know I've done my job for them, they're happy. I'm happy because I got them and that they're being great.

EPC: It sounds like it. How do you differentiate yourself from other celebrity event planners?

Katrina: You know that old expression don't look back because they could gain on you? I try not to even look at other sites, especially the guy I used to work for who keeps popping up like a bad penny no matter how many lawsuits he's had, and of course, I won't name him. I know my people come back year after year and that's my business is repeat business. I do full service, I negotiate and book, I work on promo. I'm very good using social media to sell tickets. I'll work with the theater every day to make sure we're selling tickets, to make sure. I have the production timeline as far as, "Okay we have lights, we have sound, we have risers, we have floor covering. This guys got to be here by this time." The piano tuner. Things you can't even think of. "We have the food drops, we have this, we have that person with allergies. Make sure they're not in the room with the other person who wants the peanut sauce." Just all kinds of things you'd never think of, and I am good with details like that.

EPC: How do you make sure the right things get done at the right time by the right people?

Katrina: It's a skill I think. I tell people a concert is like a wedding except it has 27 brides, because you have all the band members and all the staff and things. I have organizers, I have Excel sheets, but I just have that ability to remember. I think working for doctors and surgeons you remember to have all the equipment in that operating room. You remember to have the schedule on his desk in the morning. You remember all the things the other demanding personalities needed, and it's just an easy carryover into celebrity work.

EPC: Are there any software programs or apps you use to manage all the details?

Katrina: I use Excel like anybody else, but not really. Believe it or not my best friend is my production binder that has pockets and things for distinct parts of the contract rider and I'll just tab over to lights, because you know what, if technology fails then you're messed up. I don't want that to happen, so I have it printed out, I carry it on the plane with me, and I can go right to lights, okay, this isn't the right light, these aren't the right filters. I have a list of phone numbers even though I have my cell phone. I have the phone numbers printed out. I'm making sure nothing can go wrong if something goes wrong. I can still recover.

EPC: What is working for you to attract new clients?

Katrina: I'm doing social media and I try to get involved with events like Event Planners, organizations like Event Planners, and I am in organizations that hospitals are in like AFP. I'm just trying to be out there all the time. I found going to conventions and just sitting in a booth has never worked for me, but I do want to come out and meet anybody who has any interest in talking about it, so I'm always looking for event planners or AFP or some other kind of event I can go to.

EPC: How do you manage the financial aspects of your business?

Katrina: Finance is a huge part of it. When I first talk to the client to see if they can even afford it, because the first call is a discovery call. I assume they're someone who hasn't done this before, there's just more questions than I can imagine. I always start and say you need to establish a budget to find out what you can afford because here are the expenses. There's the talent fee, there's related expenses. Air fare for the whole entourage and band, food, instrument rental, venue, insurance, security, just everything in the rider you can imagine.

I want them to know all the expenses ahead of time. Once they know what they can afford, if they can afford it, I ask them for what that number is just for the talent fee and what genre they want. I run them a custom list in their genres under the fee. I say here are the people you can afford, and that's how we start picking so we make sure we stay within their expenses.

EPC: How do you manage the ups and downs of the business where one month you might have a ton of events and the next month might be a little bit slower?

Katrina: Right now, this is my busy time. I'm on planes almost every weekend, and that's fun for me and I love it. Then I don't know how to act for the first few weekends when it's the dead of winter and nobody wants to have an event. I still have people who are planning for next year. I still have plenty of five-days-a-week work to do. I just go down to five days from seven.

EPC: What's the best advice you've ever gotten?

Katrina: I think probably the best advice I've gotten is from me when I worked for someone else and I told myself always be honest. I mean it's too much trouble to lie and cover and do what the previous employer I had did. Just be honest. It's so much easier and so much nicer and you don't have to worry about anything.

EPC: That is great advice. For our listeners who are resonating more, are resonating with what you're saying and want to learn more about all things Katrina where is the best place for them to go? Tartantalent.com?

Katrina: Exactly. Tartan. By the way I thought when I chose the name of my business I thought everyone knew who Tartan was, what it was, and apparently, they don't. Tartan is a kind of plaid and I'm Scottish, so I thought it was a cute name. It turns out I shouldn't have gotten that one because people don't know. It's T-A-R-T-A-N talent dot com.

Katrina: Here are some of my secret insights:
I'll talk with people about their entire gala as far as working with the celebrity to get silent auction items. I can tell them extra ways to raise money like sell backstage passes with a professional photographer so your head sponsor or your big donor can have a picture in his office of himself with the celebrity he helped underwrite. That goes a huge way.

EPC: Thanks to Katrina McGregor of TartanTalent.com.

EPC Book Recommendation:

You'll Never Eat Lunch in This Town Again
by Bernie Brillstein

CHAPTER 13
DJ Nahchey
Dash Entertainment

At the Event Planners Club, we identify what makes experts like Nahchey so unique. He found DJ Mixing to be his heartbeat, and leverages his banker roots to run the business.

EPC: Welcome DJ Nahchey of Dash Entertainment in Los Angeles. What inspired you to go into the event planning industry?

Nahchey: Well, it was a little bit of necessity mixed with a desire to be a DJ. In a former life, I worked for Deutsche Bank in finance. When I got laid off I decided to take a big chance and enter the world of club DJs, which I did for about four or five years. During that time, I realized that I needed to have a backup plan in case I didn't become a superstar DJ, so I started an entertainment booking agency on the side which basically became Dash Entertainment. I started the company as a side project and then it ended up taking over and became more of a career for me than my DJing. Now, I still DJ, but mostly I run the company.

EPC: Okay. Obviously, you have the DJ background but as far as event planning, is there a specific area of expertise that you have?

Nahchey: I'm not an event planner, I'm involved with the Event Planner's Association as well as several other networking groups that involve event planners. It's more of the production side of things, where we do sound and lighting production as well as hire talent for large corporate events. About, probably, 70% of our business is weddings, entertainment, and sound, and lighting production for weddings.

EPC: As you have gone along, everything isn't always perfect along the way. Have you made a mistake along the way, that you look back and go "Oh, wish I hadn't done that?" Or flip-side of it is "Boy, I made that mistake but look what I learned from it and look what it's produced for me since then."

Nahchey: Yeah, there's been lots of small things that I've learned, kind of the hard way or just by making little mistakes along the way. A lot of it, collecting final payments two weeks prior to the event instead of on the night of the event. Really making sure that your contracts are air tight, because there have been a few instances, here and there, where people have tried to cancel or get out of contracts that had already been paid for. A few things like that. I've had my taste of small claims court and, lucky for me, we won that case and now we have airtight contracts with insurance. Little things like that, along the way.

EPC: You really had to learn how to be a businessman?

Nahchey: Yes. How to run a small business, I kind of learned it on my own. My background is economics and I used to work for Deutsche Bank doing macroeconomic research, not small business type stuff. I had to learn how to, you know, it's not just dipping into bank account and paying myself a salary, and hire a real accountant that can keep the books for me, because my version of keeping the books was getting sloppy. I had to learn a lot about networking. I had to learn how to become a salesperson, which I'm not by nature. When you run a small business, you end up doing just about a little bit of everything.

EPC: Tell me what you think makes a successful event.

Nahchey: I think food and music are the two most important things.

EPC: You're a little biased.

Nahchey: I'm a little biased, I agree. Venues are important, as well but people very rarely leave an event talking about the drapery, or maybe the flowers but not so much. If the music's great and the food's great, people are going to talk about it and they're going to remember that. I like to do events where we go over-the-top, where we have a DJ accompanied by live musicians that jam with them live, and we have great lighting effects and a very produced show. It's not for everyone but that's what I like to do. Small events with just one performer are great and it's probably our bread and butter, but what's fun for me is putting together the big shows.

EPC: What do you like best about what you do?

Nahchey: I'm a huge music fan, so just being able to

constantly be exposed to new music and new talent is probably the most fun for me. In a former life, I played it safe by going into finance, but my heart was never really in it. I always wanted to do something with music, so taking my chance to be a DJ was kind of my way to get involved in the music industry, without necessarily having the training of a musician. Now, I really don't look back and I really have no regrets about stepping away from finance and going into this.

EPC: Flip side of that, what drives you crazy about the business?

Nahchey: What drives me crazy is that it's a constant hustle. You can never just kick back and rest on your royals and start counting your money, because invariably the industry is in such flux all the time, people come and go so rapidly. You might have 20 or 30 amazing event planners and venues that recommend you all the time, but those people turn over and if you don't constantly continue to hustle, you're going to start fading away as well. You can never stop selling yourself. You can never stop hustling. If you want to grow, you have to work, I think, twice as hard as other industries, just because there's so much turnover and people go away, and people forget about you, and you really, really have to stay in front of people and on their minds in order to be successful. It's a constant hustle. I wish I could get to a point where I could just kick back and watch the gigs and the money roll in, but I don't think that's ever going to happen.

EPC: You're still doing what you do. You're doing what

you love. You started your own business, you have built it, it's here. That alone makes you successful, the fact that you're still around. This is going to sound like a cliché question, but what do you attribute your success to?

Nahchey: First, I started the company kind of like a niche market to find wedding couples and clients that were interested in slightly edgier entertainment than what was out there. Being a club DJ and coming from the world of electronic music, I wanted to find people that liked that genre of music as well. We really started off as a niche company, using real turntables, and using real DJs to perform as opposed to what the industry was doing at the time, which is just kind of a guy that's popped in and out CDs, or played mp3s off a computer, that wasn't very interesting. Having a specialty and being a little different from the rest of the pack, I think, initially helped distinguish us.

Then, just being hungry and not giving up. You must get out there and network. You must perform. You must take every gig that comes your way, initially anyway, before you start being pickier and choosing about what you will and won't do. Just really being tenacious, I guess, is probably the reason for our success. Also, having a personality that makes it easy for people to work with you. I know there's a lot of DJs that are prima donnas or really set in their own ways, you get a client that really doesn't like working with them, because they make their life the priority. I've always tried to be super easy going, super accommodating, leave my attitude at home and not try to really push my personal musical tastes on people, but really figure out what they want and give them what they want.

It's a mixture of more than one thing, but I would say, being flexible and easy to work with is huge because I hear a lot of other clients complain about people that aren't. Then, it's just working hard.

EPC: What's your biggest challenge right now?

Nahchey: My biggest challenge right now, is getting to the next level. It's easy to plateau. You make these pushes and then you stop growing and you tend to stay at the same levels for a little while. Right now, what we're exploring, is getting involved and finding new revenue streams, renting out photo booths and booking other kinds of talent. We want to get DJs that play dance and specialty musicians, like electronic violinists and things like that. Now, we're pushing a little bit into photo booths and eventually, videographers and the photography world. I think to continue growing you really have to find new revenue streams and new things to do and you have to do different things as well. Some of the things we've been exploring a lot lately is combining DJs with live musicians. That's always a big hit.

EPC: Okay. As you add new things to your entourage here, part of that is, of course, using vendors and they're not just people that work for you. You bring in outside people.

Nahchey: Exactly.

EPC: How do you evaluate the vendors? What challenges are you facing in finding the right mix there?

Nahchey: First, usually, I will be out and about either in the "club world" or "special event world" and finding talent that way, or often, we get contacted by talent that is looking for representation. I would say, nine out of ten of them we're not interested in, or they're not a right fit. The first thing that talent needs to have is really, good headshot, bios, and especially videos. It's almost impossible for us to sell new talent to clients without video and demo reels these days. That's kind of the first thing we look at.

            Then, after that, it's a meeting and it's a personality evaluation just to see what their personality is like and how you think they're going to behave with your event planners that you send them to, because I've had some people that were talented, then you meet them in person, they're shifty. They can't look you in the eyes. They make you feel uncomfortable and you don't want to send anybody out like that. The next step is a personality step and then after that I always like to see them performing live somewhere.

            If that all goes well, we make an agreement with them to either represent them exclusively, or represent them as a free agent where they're free to work with anybody else that they want to. In some cases, if it's a band, you have to re-brand them. In other cases, if they have a DJ name that's already recognizable, we would have to use the first name because clients sometimes they'll try to circumvent the agent and go straight to the talent, so we must be clever as well. Excuse me. That's kind of the process that we go through for evaluating and signing new talent.

EPC: You talked earlier, about early on, learning the business aspect of running a business. How do you manage the financial aspects of it now? Are you still doing this on your own? Do you have some help?

Nahchey: Early last year I got a business coach and learned all the things that I was doing wrong and what I needed to do to start doing more, as they are done in/by real corporations instead of a mom and pop company. I outsourced our payroll. I outsourced our accounting. I got a full-time assistant. It's really freed me up to focus more on big picture stuff and not getting bogged down with maintaining the books and answering every single email. I'm on the phone with potential clients or meeting with potential clients or putting together projects for big ideas, as opposed to, doing the nitty gritty stuff now. That's been a great leap and a great transition and I think that's going to definitely help us out in the future.

EPC: Where do most of your clients come from?

Nahchey: I would say it's 40/40 between directly being referred by event planners and also directly being referred by venues, where we are on their preferred vendor list. To a lesser extent the other 20% comes from our Yelp profile, we have a nice

Yelp page with good reviews, then we get some people that find us via Google or other blogs or online forms of advertising. Really, my experience has been, most online advertising doesn't work super well and you tend to get the tire kickers and the budget. The people that are planning their own weddings, budget brides looking for deals and cheap talent. Our focus is on network and marketing to event planners and venues, because that's repeat business instead of one time sale to a bride.

EPC: For these people that you're networking with and all of that and that you hope to give referrals to you, what's your ideal client?

Nahchey: Our ideal client is a youngish couple, but not too young. They're already professionals for four to eight years in their late twenties to early thirties. I don't want to call them hipsters, but they are well traveled, well educated, they're already financially stable and they are looking for something a little more cutting edge. A little different from a traditional sort of wedding entertainment. They're doing something little grittier, a little urban, or a little fancier than most brides and grooms out there. We target as much as possible the higher end of the market.

EPC: Anyone that would like to learn more about you should do what?

Nahchey: They should go to dashentertainment.com. They can check out my profile. I have multitudes, many, many, many of my mixed tapes, demo mixes that

I've created over the years. We have profiles of all of our bands and DJs, live entertainers, and pretty much explains everything we do.

EPC: Excellent. We have been talking with Nahchey from Dash Entertainment. Thank you for taking the time to talk to us today.

EPC Book Recommendation:

When to Jump: If the Job You Have Isn't the Life You Want by Mike Lewis, foreword by Sheryl Sandberg

---

LEARNING
is GROWING.

CHAPTER 14
Shantay Parker
Sunflower Event Planning

At the Event Planners Club, we identify what makes experts like Shantay so unique. She can transform your DIY wedding into a turnkey experience on a small budget.

EPC: Shantay Parker of sunflowereventplanning.com has an inspiring story of becoming an event planner.

Shantay: It started with me doing events and planning for family and friends in the community. After doing that for a little while, I was fortunate to be able to help someone with a wedding, who didn't have quite a lot of money. Their finances weren't big, so I helped them out and assisted them with the things that I had and knew some people that are in the industry that like to help other people. We put this wedding on for them, and then after that I decided that it was something that I wanted to pursue because I knew that I could help people with big budgets and small budgets.

EPC: How did you get from there to this point in your career?

Shantay: Just pretty much doing the same thing, being able to offer my services to everyone and not turning anyone away because they don't have the finances to be able to do like a wedding, per se.

EPC: You mentioned weddings. Do you have a specific area of event planning expertise?

Shantay: Not necessarily. I pretty much can plan for just about any event. Weddings are my biggest clientele, so I do a lot of weddings, but I also do other things such as anniversary parties, birthday parties, corporate events, and things of that nature.

EPC: What are some of the biggest event planning mistakes you see clients making, and how do you help them avoid those?

Shantay: I can say the biggest mistakes that some of my clients make are trying to plan the event on their own when they're not able to handle a lot of stress, because with planning comes a lot of stressful situations. You have a lot of tasks to be done. I think a lot of my clients make the mistake of trying to plan on their own and not have a support system. I feel like if you have a support system, it's great that you can plan on your own, but if you don't handle stress very well, I think it's a better option to hire someone on who can assist you with the planning process.

EPC: That makes a lot of sense. How do you measure a successful event?

Shantay: I say a successful event is an event that where we get everything done and all the client's wishes. I would say we like to put, we call it, a spin on things. We take the client's likes, and we mix it with a little bit of our expertise. Then we get this appealing design. I'd say a successful wedding is where the bride is happy, the groom is happy, and everything goes according to plan.

EPC: What do you like best about your business?

Shantay: I love the challenges. Each client comes with a challenge as far as design plan, and they always are good at making me work my creativity side to give them what they want and what they need. I really love that part of my job.

EPC: What do you attribute your success to?

Shantay: I think my success comes from my clients. If it wasn't for my clients allowing me the opportunity to help them with their event, I don't think that I would be able to have made it thus far. I would say most of my success is attributed to my clients.

EPC: With all the success you've achieved, what's your biggest challenge now?

Shantay: I would say my biggest challenge right now is educating brides and grooms and that hiring on a party planner is not always a bank-breaker. It's not always going to cost you an arm and a leg. That's what a lot of the reasons why people try to do it themselves, because they think it's so expensive, and so they don't even give us a try. I think that's one of the biggest challenges. A lot of people like to go the do it themselves route, and I think that's a challenge for us trying to prove to them that we can help you, and not only help you, but help you save money as well.

EPC: That makes a lot of sense. Where do most of your clients come from?

Shantay: I'd say a lot of them come from all over. We get a lot of internet-based clients. We get a lot of word-of-mouth from our past clients who recommend us to other people. I would say they come from a majority of everywhere.

EPC: How do you manage the financial aspects of your business?

Shantay: Mainly with our business partners, which are a lot of the vendors that we work with. We work together in helping each other with rentals and things like that, so it helps my business and my clients save a lot of money.

EPC: What are some of the challenges you face when sourcing entertainment or vendors for your clients?

Shantay: Sometimes, the challenge we face is certain dates are booked, so when we can't work with our vendors, we have to find outside vendors. That can sometimes be a challenge because we're not 100% sure how great that vendor is. We always tell our clients, "We would like for you to talk to the vendors as well, so you can get an idea of how good or how great that vendor is as well."

EPC: Who is an ideal client for you?

Shantay: I would say an ideal client would be anyone who's looking just for any type of help with their planning process, anyone who's in the beginning of planning, in the middle of planning, or close to the end of planning but just needs a little assistance. We pretty much don't really have a set type of client because all our clients come from all different walks, are in different areas and different processes of the party planning. We pretty much treat all our clients the same no matter how much they're spending with our company.

EPC: What is the first step you would want that ideal client to take to start the process with you?

Shantay: First, I like to talk to them and see what exactly they want and need for their coming event, and then we will give them ideas on things that we can do to possibly help their event. Then from there, we usually have a sit-down meeting. If we talked to them via phone, we'll have a sit down meeting face-to-face and show them some ideas. We have a booklet, or we can bring photos or something of that nature to show them ideas of things that they can possibly do or colors and things of that nature. Then after that, we sit down with the clients, and we sign a contract so that they're guaranteed 100% that we're there at their event and that they have booked us for their event.

EPC: What else do you want people to know that I didn't think to ask you?

Shantay: I'll say, I would like people to know that we are different from any other event planning company because we are able to help people with any size budget. We have not yet had to turn a client away because of finances. We work with our clients as far as a payment arrangement; payment plans to fit it into their budget and their financial schedule. We do whatever that we can to make sure that we're able to book an event planner for their event.

EPC: Shantay Parker of sunflowereventplanning.com, specializes in wedding events with a small budget.

EPC Book Recommendation:

A Practical Wedding Planner: A Step-by-Step Guide to Creating the wedding You Want with the Budget You've Got (without Losing Your Mind in the Process) by Meg Keene

Make today the HAPPIEST day of your life!

CHAPTER 15
Yogi Patel
Global Photography

At the Event Planners Club, we identify what makes experts like Yogi so unique. Yogi is a Master award-winning photographer who has captured every culture in South Asia.

EPC: Yogi Patel of globalphotography.net has over 30 years of professional photography experience. He holds a BA in photography from the University of Florida along with a certified professional photographers' degree and a Masters in craftsman and photography from the Professional Photographers of America. Some of his images have been selected for national exhibition by the Professional Photographers of America including twice for the Prestigious Lung Collection. His work as also been published in national and international magazines.

EPC: It is our pleasure. Let's go back in time a little bit. Where did you grow up?

Yogi: I grew up in India completing my primary schooling, then I spent time in Africa before moving to Florida to study photography. I received my Bachelors in photography then worked for a photographer for five years. I moved to California to open my global photography business.

153

EPC: What inspired you to be a photographer?

Yogi: Even as a child, I loved being an artist. I used to paint a lot of paintings, oil paintings and watercolor paintings. And then from there, art took me forward and I always wanted to become a photographer from my childhood.

EPC: You talked a little bit about the geographic around the world journey, from India to Africa to Florida to California. There's lots and lots of photographers, what do you feel it is about your work that makes it stand out so much?

Yogi: First, photography is not just a camera that just takes pictures, it is your eye and your heart you put into the image. It's the way you see it, the way you liked it, and how you present the image. The finished product is what makes the difference from a good photographer to an average one. Understanding of the lighting, and understanding of posing, understanding of the full start to finish image. What makes me different from some of the others, is the time I put into creating an image and making it right. It's not just snap a shot and whatever comes out I just give it to you.

EPC: You have some absolutely stunning images on display on your portfolio on your website at globalphotography.net, talk a little bit about your expertise in South Asian weddings.

Yogi: I have been shooting South Asian weddings for the last about 16-18 years. When I moved into the market I did not shoot any thousand-year weddings, I was strictly doing bar mitzvahs and Jewish weddings and so called "Caucasian American White weddings," and Chinese weddings. About 18 years ago things changed and one of my vendors that we used to work with brought me a huge client from Hong Kong and that was my turning point. I saw the potential in the South Asian market and from there on, year after year it moved upscale and we've just gone up.

The last few years we have been awarded California Photographers of the Year award. I've also won top wedding photographer for California, awarded by Professional Photographers of California. Then understanding the culture, I am Indian, so I do understand the various parts of Indian culture, different ceremonies, different allegiances. If you know India from north to south, there are multiple cultures. And not every ceremony is the same and not every wedding is the same. So, understanding the culture gives you a leg up on somebody who doesn't know and just wants to go and shoot an Indian wedding. Being right place at the right time is important when you're shooting an Indian wedding. Also understanding how the family takes a significant role in the culture, where it is just not taking pictures of bride and groom alone. Bride and groom with their parents, bride and groom with uncle aunts, bride and groom with people who have come to their wedding from all over the world. It is very important for a couple to make sure the photographer captures all of them. This is not just about decorations, it is just not about pictures of bride and groom only.

Also understanding every aspect of the ceremony. Normally the ceremonies run anywhere from hour, hour and a half, sometimes two hours. Everything that happens in the ceremony has a meaning. If you don't know the meaning of the ceremony, if you don't understand what the priest is saying and what ceremony is going to happen, you might miss out. It's going to backfire on you later and when the client is going to come looking for those images and those important moments are not captured. So, understanding a culture is very important. Then performing, giving the client a super product at the end, is also very important.

EPC: Absolutely. Now obviously understanding the market, understanding the culture, and the language, you talk about being in the right place at right time for the ceremony. But, you've been in the right place at the right time as well. So how did it go from the first South Asian wedding that you did from Hong Kong to growing to the significant percentage of a business that it is now? How did you get that word out?

Yogi: I was in the right place at the right time as you say, but I did work very hard to get there. It just did not come in nor did anyone give me my business on a platter. I had to put in my time to learn photography, understand photography first. I have a double Masters in Photography, and a fellowship in photography. Not that everybody who wants to know photography has to have all those degrees, but those degrees do help in your work.

Also, the way I got into where I am now, I did start where I did not know anything about Indian wedding photography, but I had to learn. I went and studied every aspect of diverse cultures that are different than my culture. I am Hindu, and I know everything about Hindu weddings and I got married in a Hindu ceremony, so I know all of it. But besides Hindu there is Punjabi weddings, Sikh weddings, Indian weddings, Mongolian weddings and so many other diverse kinds that I had to go study and understand what happens at them all. Shooting more and more and more and more, in 18 years, I've probably shot every different culture there is out there. Talking to your clients in the initial stages, if you want to get into the market, the more research you do, more you talk to your clients and get the feel of what the client wants, and be prepared to deliver what the client wants, is what will bring you ahead of the other guys.

My marketing is solely word of mouth. It was the product, we gave it to our clients, and they referred us to other people. And other people, their friends, their family members saw our albums, and they were really impressed with it, so this is how the business grew. And still today, our business is all word of mouth. The past clients are important to us, those are our bread and butter and we do definitely do anything that a client would - we will bend over backwards to keep our clients happy.

EPC: That makes a lot of sense. How do you measure a successful wedding?

Yogi: How do I measure a successful wedding? The measurement of successful wedding would be how happy your clients are. As far as your clients are happy with what you've given them, and you have done a little more than what they had expected you, that would be your measure. It is the clients who must agree and speak for you, I cannot brag myself. I can tell everything what I do and what I've done but my measure of my success would come from my clients. That is how I would see it. If my clients are happy, if the community is speaking well about our work, if the vendors are speaking well about what we do, that would be my measurement of my work. It won't be just me telling how good I am.

EPC: Absolutely. What are you finding are some of the biggest mistakes that brides and grooms make when trying to choose a wedding photographer?

Yogi: The biggest mistake a bride and groom will make is not meeting with the photographer personally. Just going by a beautiful looking website and deciding, "Well I like the pictures on the website so that'll be my photographer." Second mistake would be judging the photographer by the price. Price should never be the factor on determining who your photographer should be because photo and video is your lifetime memory. No matter how much money you have to spend on your flowers, your decorations, or your food, everything is just for that few hours of that day. Rest of the lifetime memories is what we are capturing. If the photographer has not captured the full spectrum of the wedding from bride getting ready, to details of her clothing, to details of her beautiful outfit that she spent so much time finding, decorations of the room, including the pictures of bride and groom, romantic shots, the family pictures, the ceremony, the full spectrum of the wedding; if it's not captured in the right way then the photographer has not done the job and no matter how much money you have spent, at the end the bride and the groom are the ones who are losing out.

There are a lot of websites that might look good, they might show you everything, but these days anybody can make their website look good. There's a lot of stock pictures we heard people are using in their website, so it is a best thing for a bride and groom to take their time, personally visit a photographer, at the studio, not at a Starbucks, not at some restaurant where you just see some pictures on a laptop. You have to make sure the photographer is established, that he's going to be there years from now to deliver your product and your family weddings. It is not like you saw somebody and tomorrow he might be gone out of business and you are looking for him. Stories we do hear in my path.

This is my 31st year, so I have heard a lot of stories. A lot of the clients get burned. They cannot find the photographer, they don't have any pictures, they already paid all the money. So, stories like this will teach a client that you should rely on the reputation of the photographer. When you're looking for a photographer do not just go by, "He is giving me the best deal." Always the best deal is not always the best for you. You should get a quote from somebody low, medium, and high and then just from there is the photographer going to give you what your expectations are? From there judge whether the money that the photographer is charging - does is justify?

Also, the end product. A lot of photographers these days just want to shoot and burn and give you the file and never want to see the clients. They do sell the client in that way. "Well you can make your own albums, you don't need a custom design album, you just need the file," which is very wrong thing because 90% of the clients don't know how to design an album.

They will get the files, they will sit on the CDs for years, and then two years down the road, they will find a photographer that can design a book for them and then say, "Well my photographer just gave me the files and I don't have an album and I don't know what to do with it. Can you design a book for us?" At that point the clients are going to end up spending more money than initially finding a photographer who can give them a full package, including their albums, including the engagement session, including portraits, including parent albums, and thank you cards, which is a complete package that any bride and groom will want. When you try to buy a la carte afterwards it always becomes expensive.

EPC: Absolutely. I think that is 100% accurate and great advice. What else do you want to share with our audience that I didn't think to ask you?

Yogi: As a wedding photographer, I would say it is a photographer's job to guide the clients. Because sometimes this is their first wedding. They don't even know what to ask or where to go. Yes, they have read a lot of stuff online or one of those wedding books where they have list of questionnaires to ask your photographer. And they have a list of photos to take like bride and groom, bride with mom, bride and dad. Which photographer would not take those pictures? If that list is not covered plus more by the photographer, there's something wrong with that photographer.

Stuff like the basic things is good for bride and groom to know but as a photographer, there's a lot of behind the scenes things that bride and groom will never expect that they should know, regarding the timings, how much time a photographer would need to create beautiful images for them. Normally a coordinator these days is into wedding planning where the photographer will always work with the coordinator and the bride and groom, and come up with a timeline that suits everybody, but sometimes coordinators do not understand and basically create a timeline for the bride and groom and give 10 minutes to take pictures of bride and groom, 10 minutes for the family, and 10 minutes for the wedding party. They want to just get it over and get on to the wedding. If a client is looking for stunning images and creating work, no photographer can give beautiful images of bride and groom in 10 minutes. And 10 minutes of photography for the family. So that's why it is the photographer's job to tell the client how much time would be required to do what they have been expected to do.

The other thing, these days, a dime a dozen, everybody is a photographer these days, especially cell phones. And people have got into this habit of instant gratification. "Well I've taken a picture on cell phone, just put it on Facebook, put it on Instagram," and we've seen it and the novelty is finished. If you go to a professional photographer, they are not shooting pictures on cell phones. They are not going to be able to take your pictures and put them on Facebook right away or next day, because they must edit their clients - clean up whatever blemishes that need to be taken care of, adjust the exposure, make the images look 10 times better than your friends and family are putting online.

As a client, you have to make sure that whatever the photographer is putting online, it would need time to do that. We are not just taking, as a photographer, 5 or 6 pictures for Facebook; yes, we do take some pictures on our cameras to instantly put it on there so that at least the clients and their friends can see them, the edited works take time. That is what the clients would be expecting from their photographer; nothing that somebody just shot it on regular JPEG format, at the end of the day, burn the CD, hand it to client without editing, without doing anything to the images, that is not a photographer's job and that is not what a photographer should do. A photographer, if he's just shooting and burning without editing, giving files to their client, they are not doing justice to their client. They are not giving their client what a client should want. Client should be provided with the finished artwork images that they can literally take and make prints to any size they want.

That is what our end product and our goal is; to give clients finished products, not something that they can just literally come in next day, take it, and put it on Facebook, and their happy with.

EPC: That is great advice, makes a ton of sense. We greatly appreciate the interview. We've been talking here with Yogi Patel of globalphotography.net. Yogi thank you so much again for joining us.

EPC Book Recommendation:

Wedding Storyteller, Volume 1: Elevating the Approach to Photography Wedding Stories
by Roberto Valenzuela

Leave
a little
SPARKLE
wherever
you go.

CHAPTER 16
Jonathan Rivera
The Podcast Factory

At the Event Planners Club, we identify what makes experts like Jonathan so unique. He's a Podcast Pro, and is turning free podcasts into a money-making machine.

EPC: Jonathan Rivera spent 10 years as an electrician, then switched to real estate where he held a million dollars in properties, lost it all, and then totally bounced back. He has an amazing hero's journey. Now he is making his mark through The Podcast Factory. Let's start there. Jonathan, tell us the impetus for starting that up.

Jonathan: You talked about how I made a million and lost a million. That hurt. After that happened, there was this low time when I lost everything. Not only did we lose all our investment properties, but eventually my house was foreclosed on. My dad's house was foreclosed on. We lost everything. About that time, my little limiting beliefs came creeping into my ear. "See, you aren't good enough. You weren't supposed to have that. Why did you think you could escape the rat race? Go back, slave." I was so close to just giving into it, but I fought back.

One of the things that helped me at that time was I had a friend who turned me on to podcasts, audio books and all that stuff. Up until that point, all I had ever studied was real estate investment techniques. I bought my first house with no money down. I did all these crazy cool investment techniques. I didn't know anything about running a business. When I got into the world of podcasts, I learned about being an entrepreneur, about sales, about positioning, about marketing. It took me on this whole other path that helped me build the foundation of the business that I have today.

It took about a decade for me to rebuild my real estate business. Now my rentals are full. I have a waiting list. Just today I turned two people down. I said, "I don't have anything for a month and a half." It's all because of this education I got starting from podcasts, moving on to other mentors. Nowadays, now that that real estate business is dialed in, I have people, systems and processes. It's all running like a machine. I have more free time. In fact, it was a year ago today, maybe a year and a day, when I decided to turn The Podcast Factory into a business. Before that, it was me talking to my buddies and sharing it with the world.

EPC: Then we should say Happy Podcastiversary. It's interesting about your journey and especially how you talked about those limiting beliefs. I know that that's something that a lot of people struggle with. Entrepreneurs, solopreneurs, people at whatever stage of business they're in. Can you talk about how you fought back against those voices? They can be so crippling, so limiting, and just stop us from really going after what we want. In your experience, what's the solution to that?

Jonathan: There is no permanent solution. The one thing that you can count on is recognizing it and working on it. I've been struggling through all layers of my business. I did well when I jumped into real estate, then I lost everything. I'm thinking, "Oh, my God I'm never going to make it again." Then I rebuilt, and I was making more than I'd ever made, more than my parents ever made, more than anybody I knew ever made. But I hit a ceiling, and now I'm thinking, "This is it. I hit another plateau. I don't even deserve to be here." I was stuck there for a while. But I had a mentor who helped me expand my mind. He used to tell me, "Think bigger. Thinking big isn't enough. Think bigger." That's my buddy Darren who's been my mentor for a very long time and is a good friend. I did the first show on The Podcast Factory Network with him.

"Think bigger." He helped me through that. I broke through that plateau. Then I hit another one a couple years later. This is what's going to happen to you as you grow, especially if you came up like me. I was raised from lower middle class and we had just enough. I was raised to believe that money was the reason that we couldn't have things. I would want something, like a pair of sneakers. My parents would say "We don't have the money. We don't have the money for that at all." I was raised with that mindset, that money was the reason I couldn't have things. Is that twisted or what? Money is the reason you CAN have things. Wake up.

Through the various stages where I've hit plateaus, where I've stalled out, where I've run into some trouble, I found the right mentors and the right people to be around, and expanded my thinking beyond what I thought my limits were before. That consistently happens. I'll hit another plateau. I haven't hit it yet this time, thank goodness. But I'll hit another one and I'll have to get around some billion-dollar players, and that's just the way it is.

EPC: Mentors are so important. It sounds like they've played a tremendous role in your success and your growth. How can people find mentors for themselves?

Jonathan: I wrote a book called *Podcast Recipes*. I'm going to share one of my recipes with you. I call this the guru love potion. The way it works is, first you have to be consistently looking for people to be your mentor because if you're not looking for them, they aren't going to find you, I promise you that. So, you spot out someone that you want to be your mentor. That could take some time depending on who you are and what networks you're in. Next thing you do, and this is the easiest part of the whole thing, you buy their product or their coaching or their consulting, whatever it is. You take money out of your pocket and invest in them. For most people that's the easy part. Here comes the hard part.

EPC: Doing it?

Jonathan: That's right. That's the hard part. Doing the work. That's where most people stall out. You have to take what they've taught you, use it and put it to work. That's when you get results. Lo and behold, results come when you do the work. What you do is you share your results with that mentor. "Hey, I used your product." I just did that myself. Two weeks ago, I bought a product called *Phone Funnels* from a buddy of mine, Ryan Stewman. I need to get on more phone calls because I do most of my sales on the phone. This came along and I said, "That's perfect. I've got to get on that." It was a thousand bucks. I dropped a thousand and didn't even think about it. I bought it on a Friday. I went to work Monday and Tuesday, going through the program, building the funnels and getting it all in place. It's been three weeks since I bought it. I've already made my first sale for two thousand dollars. I covered all my costs. I covered all my investment. I went back to Ryan and said, "Oh, God, check it out. I got my investment back. I got all this stuff back."

Is he going to take in interest in that? He's going to say, "My stuff works. Here's my poster boy." That's how you do it. You just prove that it works and that's how you start getting close to them. You do that enough times, people are going to say, "Come here, son. Let me take you under my wing. Let me show you a little something." That's how I get mentors. That's my guru love potion. They fall in love with you because you're just proving that they're as awesome as they think they are.

EPC: It's so hard to do the work, but once you do and you get the results, it's so worth it. When you can find those relationships with those mentors, boom, there's your recipe right there.

Jonathan: Yes.

EPC: One of the unique and interesting things you do is you create video sales letters for your rental properties. That's probably one of the reasons that you are booked out. You have no openings available. Can you share a little bit about how event planners can take that approach? Maybe make a parallel between event planners and their business and what you've done with your video sales letters and your real estate business.

Jonathan: The main thing with anything you do, event planners, real estate, podcasting, anything, the main thing you need to know is your market. You need to know how they think, what keeps them up at night, what they want out of life. You need to know as much as you can about your market. If you start there, you almost can't fail.

              The problem is, most people won't spend the time doing the research because there's not something tangible from research except pages of notes. There's nothing out there. Most of us are impatient and we want something out there. But doing the research to get to know your market is the most important thing. Talking about my rentals, it took me years get to know them, get to know my customers, get to have a deeper understanding of what troubled them, what was most attractive about my offer to them, and just talking to them and getting feedback.

              That goes with event planning. I use that same process when I'm starting a podcast show. Just getting to know the market. An event planner would do the same thing. Who is the market? It's a certain type of event you're planning. So, who is your market? Get to know them. Get to know their pain. Then you can use any one of these tactics. Use a video sales letter, a written sales letter, a Facebook ad. These are all tactics. Behind the tactics is the underlying need that your market has. Knowing that need, then you can apply the tactics in a better way. For instance, what I understood about my market after many years of talking to them and getting to know them is I'm one of them, because the apartments I have would be perfect for me if I was still a blue-collar worker. I'd think they were the best thing in the world.

The thing is, I knew the market. I knew a credit check was a problem. I knew a big down payment was a problem. I knew rents going up was a problem. I knew repairs not getting done in a timely manner was a problem. I knew these were all problems they had. I worked that into my video sales letter and my sales funnel in multiple ways, whether it was on the letter, whether it was in the email I sent, whether it was in the FAQs, I used that knowledge of my market and put it all together to connect with them and answer their pains and their needs before they brought them up to me. It was almost like I was reading their minds. That's what they love. They're saying, "You know me better than I know myself. You're my pal. Thank you."

EPC: What's the best way somebody can really get to know you? It's the deep stuff, not the stuff that people are going to talk about in surface level conversation. You have to go one step deeper. You have to go below, "It's just too much money. It takes an effort to move. I didn't like the house." It's that stuff in here that is problematic. How do you go one step deeper and really get to those deeper fears that drive people, or prevent them from acting, or to speak to what's really going on for them?

Jonathan: If we're running our own business, we're sales people at some point. I consider myself a salesman. The problem is that most people think about sales as, "I'm talking." They're talking about their benefits. They're talking about what they do. They talk, talk, talk. The secret to being a better salesperson is simple. Learn to listen. You have to learn to listen. You ask a question.

I'll give you another. This is not in the *Podcast Recipes* book. People paid me for this. I might get in trouble for sharing it. It's Snow White's secret to making people love you. It's the idea of the mirror. You may have heard of Dr. Robert Cialdini and his theories on influence. People like people who are like them. That mirroring technique. The ALR formula is Ask, Listen, and Repeat. The remarkable thing is when you ask and when you listen, and then you repeat in a concise manner like you've processed the information and you have a more distilled, tighter version of what they just told you, they're saying, "God, you know me so well."

If you want to know your market, you could do all those superficial things. Going to forums, Facebook groups, all that. That's fine at the surface level. But you want to go to that deeper level that you and I are talking about. You have to get in there. You have to talk to your market. In fact, if you can make it a point to talk to at least one person in your market every day and use the ALR formula, you're going to know them better than they know themselves inside of the next six months.

EPC: What I'm hearing you say is that it's very important to ask, listen to what they have to say and then repeat it back to them.

Jonathan: That's exactly right. Then people feel like you want to be the most popular person in the room, you'll know me at a networking event, which I don't go to many. You'll know me at a networking event if you never met me before, you'll know me because you'll be talking to me for 20 minutes and then you'll be like, "Gosh, I've just been talking forever. Tell me something about you." I'll be like, "No, I know enough. Good to meet you." I'll repeat some stuff back to them or circle the conversation back to them. You will know nothing about me. I will know everything about you.

EPC: You'll be their favorite person.

Jonathan: I will be the most popular person in the room.

EPC: Networking is so important for event planners. I see the crossover here where if they just take one thing away from this, it's just to ask and to listen. Ask and listen, whether it's a potential client, a partner, a vendor, whoever it is, just ask and just listen.

Jonathan: I'm going to make a book suggestion. It's *The Dan Sullivan Question* by Dan Sullivan. It's a very thin book and an easy read. It gives you this question structure. It's called the R-Factor question and the DOS conversation. If you follow that and you have those conversations with your customers and your clients, you're going to have a much deeper understanding of them today, of where they're going and of how you can be of service to them. That's one of the things I'm doing now.

I was running a lot of Facebook ads for the last six months. I've been running tons of Facebook ads. Then I realized, this cold traffic doesn't work for what I'm doing. They're going to buy little products here and there, but I have high-ticket stuff for sale. The cold traffic just doesn't work for me. What I did was I invested time into my customers with this conversation, the R-factor conversation. It makes them feel good because you're asking them a lot of questions, you're listening and you're repeating. That's great. It also opens them up because it's a dialogue where they're going toward what they want in their future. They're going to tell you what's holding them back. They're going to tell you what their strengths are.

Then you can look at that. And this is what any good salesperson does. They ask a lot of questions to get a better understanding of the person they're talking to. Then they look at their product and see if they can make a connection. When you have those discussions, the R-Factor discussions, you're going to get all this information that you wouldn't have ever gotten before. I'm not talking one or two layers deep, we're going many layers, down to their root dreams. What are your dreams in three years? I had one person I didn't even know. He really wanted to be more physically fit. I sent him some information on being physically fit. I had another guy that said he wanted to do more volunteer work. I sent him a book that I thought was great for what he wanted to do. You start connecting the dots. Even if it isn't for your business right now, it's being of service to them and building a longer-term bond.

EPC: Being of service and building that long-term bond. Even if they're not your client today or tomorrow, maybe they are a year from now, or maybe they know somebody who could be a potential fit. It's really about making those real connections that last over time and not saying, "You can't help me. See you later."

Jonathan: There are certain people to do that with. I would recommend that. I'm in the *Strategic Coach* program and I've learned you'll have your top 20 people who are responsible for your income in the next 90 days. Those are the people you start with. With event planners, it's who you have or have had events or multiple events with. Start with those people. Dig in and start being of service because they've already proven that they're going to hire you. They've proven that they can pay you and they've proven that they're going to work with you. Start with those people. Have that deeper conversation. That will lead to more business.

EPC: Let me ask you about what you've seen podcasting do for other people. It's not necessarily a means to a successful business in and of itself. It's just a tool, right? I'm sure you're better equipped than anybody that we're talking to, to talk about what good podcasting could do for somebody in any industry.

Jonathan: For the most part, people are delusional about podcasts. The thing is, podcasts are not going to make you famous. You're more than likely not going to land a big sponsorship deal. A podcast itself is not a business. But a lot of people jump in and think they can turn the podcast into a business. They can't do that. What a podcast excels at, where it shines above any other piece of content, is time. The average person will look at a blog maybe 90 seconds. Look at your bounce rates on your website. If you get 90 seconds, you're probably happy. Most people get less than that. If you look at videos, the average video user is watching maybe an hour or two of video a month. I'm talking about YouTube videos and stuff like that. Not Netflix. They'll just binge out on that.

But the average podcast listener, according to Edison Research, spends five hours per day listening to podcasts. Talk about an advantage. Being in someone's ear. I mean, how much closer can you get to the brain? You're talking right to their brain. What podcasts excel at is a conversion tool. You have a person on your list or a prospect or somebody out there who could be a customer, and you have your products over here for sale, and you have your podcast here in between where they don't know if they want to buy from you. Then you send them to the podcast and they get to spend some time with you because usually they're going to listen to you on their commute, while they're at the gym, while they're doing different stuff. They'll commit to a good 20-30 minutes. What other piece of content are people spending 20 or 30 minutes on? If it isn't a sitcom, it's probably not happening. The podcast excels there, where you get to have that connection, that time and that conversion.

EPC: You must have some commonality between each of your shows, right?

Jonathan: Sometimes my clients get mad at me about this, but I warn them before they sign up and give me all the money, that they're going to have to some homework. So, the way I start with them is before we record a show, before we do anything, we spend the whole first week with them drilling into their market, everything they know about their market, everything they know about their best buyers, all that kind of stuff to get their mind primed. A lot of times they say, "Do I need to do this work?" I must push them through that because then it makes them think. It gets them real clear. It gets them real focused on their market, on their market's problems so then in week two when we go into production, they know what to talk about because they just spent the whole first week thinking about their market. The topics need to line up with their market, what their market needs and what their goals are for the show because, for me, the podcast is just a bridge between your email lists and your cash register. That's all it is.

EPC: You still need to do the work. There's no substitute for the work. One of the things we talk a lot about is grit. For the entrepreneur, it's getting into the ring and showing up and continuing to work. Just chip away at stuff whether it's uncomfortable or hard or challenging, or you're butting up against those limiting beliefs or the upper limit that you're experiencing. There's just no substitute for that, right?

Jonathan: You are 100% correct. It's that grit, that being able to show up every day. People ask me, "What's your super power?" Whenever they ask me that I say, "Showing up every day." Whether it was 1000 degrees in the Florida sun turning wrenches, being an electrician. Whether it's dealing with foreclosures and short sales as a real estate agent. Or whether it's just working through my podcast stuff and all the grind. It's just showing up every day making just a little bit of progress so that at least I keep moving. That's my super power. I could show up every day. I'm relentless and that really comes down to grit.

EPC: It's those entrepreneurs or solopreneurs who are willing to just go at it day in and day out and keep it up regardless, right?

Jonathan: Absolutely right.

EPC: I know you had a friend, Big Frank, who gave you some advice that never left you.

Jonathan: When I was still an electrician, I moved to Maryland. I had a girlfriend who became a flight attendant. We moved to Maryland because that's where their hub was. She was gone all the time. I had to find some new friends. I had a couple buddies that I related to who reminded me of some of the people I grew up with when I was a kid in the Bronx. I was hanging out in some very weird areas. If you've ever seen *The Wire*, there are these really rough areas of Baltimore that are run down and boarded up. I'd be driving through those areas and hanging out two or three blocks away with Big Frank, and the rest of the gang over there.

I was lucky to be there around those guys because they always looked out for me. I never felt like there was ever any problem with me being there. Although, if I wasn't there with them, maybe there would have been. Whenever the kids would act up, whenever anybody would get out of line, Big Frank kept control of his little area. He was a cool guy. They'd be acting up and he'd just step up and say, "You going to do something? Don't talk about it. Be about it. Don't talk about it. Be about it." I heard that. "Don't talk about it. Be about it." That just stayed in my head till this day, in fact, I write it. I have this thing called The Success Journal I use every day and one of the things is Thought of the Day. That comes up still all the time. "Don't talk about it. Be about it."

You want to launch a podcast? Don't talk about it. Be about it. You want to be a successful event planner? Don't talk about it. Be about it. You want to be a best-selling author? Don't talk about it. Be about it. That advice has never left me. But it's funny where it came from to where it is today in my head.

EPC: I'm going to write it on my little note pad next to me. It's such a beautifully succinct way to get right to the point. Don't talk about it. Be about it. Thanks, Big Frank.

Jonathan: That's all you've got to do.

EPC: Jonathan, tell everyone where they can get in touch with you.

Jonathan: I've put together 10 of my best podcast recipes. That includes the "no money down" podcast recipe to launch a show without any money down. It includes the "guru love potion". It's 10 of my best podcast recipes. They're available to anyone who downloads the *Podcast Factory* app. Just text "factory" to 44222 and I'll send you a link. You can download the app. When you open it up, you can find the 10 podcast recipes right there on the front page and download it. It's a PDF. You'll get the app, you'll get the podcast recipes, plus you'll get the other shows on the networks and interviews. That's all inside the app.

EPC: Thank you so much. I really appreciate your time and sharing all those secrets that you didn't expect to reveal to all of us. Thank you for lending us your time. Which is really your most valuable resource.

EPC Book Recommendation:

Jonathan's downloadable eBook, *Podcast Recipes*

CHAPTER 17
Carol Trapschuh
GBS Linens

At the Event Planners Club, we identify what makes experts like Carol so unique. She inventories various quality products to match her varying customers' segments and budgets.

EPC: Carol Trapschuh of GBSLinens.com has some key learnings.

Carol: Well, thank you for the invitation, I appreciate it.

EPC: Where did you grow up?

Carol: I grew up in Bryan, Ohio, a Midwestern country girl. My grandparents were farmers and I attended a small school, graduating class of 100. Can you believe that, being out here in California where there's thousands to a class. I grew up, got married, moved to Cincinnati, Ohio, Washington D.C. and then I was transferred out to California where I had the good luck to eventually meet my current employer, GBS Linens.

EPC: What did you do before GBS Linens?

Carol: My very first sales job was at 25. That was a real learning curve for me because I wasn't prepared. I was in Washington D.C., living in Maryland, and I had to cover five states. I was traveling four out of five days per week. I had to really throw myself into a new life of selling on the road. That's a time where there weren't a lot of women traveling and staying in hotels on the road. It was a little uncomfortable, but I got used to it.

I was selling automotive aftermarket products for import car dealerships, like sheepskin seat covers and mats for the floor that had emblems, like the Porsche emblem or things like that.

I was working Philadelphia, D.C., Virginia, West Virginia and Dover. That kept me busy and on the road.

Then I was transferred to California with a company D&E Enterprises. Later I left to work for a company called Denmat, also in the automotive aftermarket. We sold the license plate frames. You know when you purchase a new car it will say, "So-and-so Mercedes-Benz" or whatever and it will say the city that it's located in. That was something I did before I joined GBS Linens.

EPC: What attracted you to GBS Linens?

Carol: I wanted to change jobs because the industry was changing, my kids were getting older, and I wanted to find something different. I answered this little, tiny ad. I mean it must have just not even an inch big. I came into GBS and that's where I met Pravin Mody, who was the owner and founder of GBS. He showed me these racks and racks of beautiful linens all stacked up and all I could think was "Oh my Gosh, this would be the best job ever." You know a lot of us women love designing décor. I was just lucky enough to start working for him back in 1996.

EPC: What do you like best about work for GBS Linens?

Carol: I like working with clients. Right now, I'm the sales manager, and before that I was the sales person. Every day in California is a beautiful, sunny, wonderful day for the most part. You would call on clients. You didn't even have appointments and they were so gracious and so welcoming. It was just a fun job because we are putting on the customer's event, so it's a happy time.

Now as a manager, I'm stuck in an office more, but I try to get out with my sales team. That was what is such an attraction--the ease of doing the business. The people that I work with are so wonderful, be it industry professionals, partners, vendors. We're all in it to produce a lovely event. I get to play because my work is with the beautiful linens. So that's the fun part for me.

EPC: Do you have a specific area of expertise?

Carol: My expertise is sales and I've been extremely successful. I consider GBS sort of the middle of the road. We're like the Nordstrom's. We try to have a excellent product line with pricing that's affordable for our clients. In the last 10 years or so, we've added nicer and nicer fabrics to compete with some of the other high-end linen clients because the industry is evolving so much differently than it was 20 years ago when I began.

Then it was like, "Give me your polyester linens. That's what I'm doing." Now you have the sequins and satin, and the specialty prints that really attract your customer. Your customer is now coming in and they want something better. They either want to design their wedding or their events. They're even willing to buy or purchase the linen.

I'm lucky because I also get to purchase linen, work with fabric vendors and try to figure out what's up and coming for the next season.

EPC: What are some of the biggest mistakes you see people making, when looking at linens for an event?

Carol: Sometimes people use too many colors. Once I had a client planning a holiday event. They wanted green and red and gold linens. That becomes overkill. You really can't tell them what to do. You just can suggest and hope they kind of get the idea. Gosh, let's put most of your colors in your flowers, but don't do more than maybe two colors of your linens. Maybe a linen and the napkins can change via assorted colors or a pattern or something like that. A lot of people try to put too much on the table and it just becomes kind of overkill.

That's where I tell my team, "Let's guide them into something where they'll be happy with the result."

EPC: What do you attribute your success and your longevity to?

Carol: I have to say a team effort is number one. The GBS management team is always willing to listen to

186

innovative ideas, and in company's that's rare, so it's really great to have that team behind me.

Plus, we have a high-quality product line that's affordable, something that we can rent, or sell. That makes it easier for the customer. Everybody can't always go high end, so we offer a range of satin fabric that's high-end to lower end so that we can accommodate customers at various price points and budget. We try to give everybody the linen they desire that they can rent from us and stay within their budget.

It's the people that you work with that are so good and it's such fun to work with them every day.

EPC   With all the success, you know the event that you've done, what would you say is your biggest challenge now?

Carol: My biggest challenge I think always is the bridal season, the wedding season. We are so, so busy because, GBS, we not only rent and do laundry for ourselves, but our customers. We all sell. We are full service. You can come into us and get almost anything. When wedding season hits, we just have so many orders. So many people want to give us those orders the day before, the night before it needs to be on the truck at the 7:00 in the morning. That is probably the biggest challenge we have. We're working on changing that process coming out a very busy season again. Changing that process to streamline it a little better. So, everybody will be a little bit happier with the outcome.

GBS has three manufacturing facilities and five other satellite stores. We are a busy growing, expanding company. We started with Anaheim almost 32 years ago and then there was Hayward, Northern California. I was instrumental in developing Arizona and Las Vegas. Our Anaheim location feeds all those stores. That means we have inter-plant trucks going up exchanging linens, giving the people linen when they have rentals and when we want to wash their linens. We are constantly feeding those stores.

In the height of the season it gets very tense trying to make sure that we can take those last-minute orders and are able to deliver them. Sometimes we can and sometimes we can't because sometimes we have a tough time saying, "No we can't do it." So, we do everything we can. That even means manufacturing at the midnight hour. That's a challenge.

EPC: Where do most of your clients come from?

Carol: The event industry, absolutely. We get our top clients from having party rental stores that do well because they come to purchase from us and then they like to rent from us. If they purchase so many colors, then they can come back to us and they can say, "I purchased 50, but I need another 25 and I know my colors will match so I'll get them from GBS Linens." If they don't have a laundry facility, then they use us to do their laundry. We're renting, turning laundry two days a week at a minimum.

Then we have hotels as clients. We do a lot of selling to hotels, a lot of rental also. We have the amazing event planners, wedding planners, and caterers. We do a lot of business with catering people. Anybody who's in the party industry--country clubs, golf clubs. We work with them.

EPC: What drives you crazy about your business?

Carol: The last minute orders. That's the hardest thing, just like I said before. We have people that will call us on 5:00 on a Wednesday, and they need something on the truck that morning. Sometimes people call you after hours and begging to get it on the truck. When that happens, we are scrambling because instead of saying, "No." We say, "Okay we'll try to do that." Now that driver that's supposed to leave at 7:00 in the morning is now leaving at 8:00. And then the route, he's got maybe 20 people, 25 people on the route. Now he's late to all his customers.

That kind of drives us crazy, but we understand that our customer has his or her customer who's calling last minute and confirming. During the busy season, that's what drives you crazy, trying to accommodate all the orders.

EPC: All right. Who is an ideal client for you?

Carol: Oh, that's easy. An ideal client is one that is satisfied and refers you. I love someone who can refer me. I've had people who refer me who didn't even do business with me because they knew of us and they knew of the services that we provide. That's perfect.

There's also the prepared client. That's the one who really understands the business. As a vendor we do our best to accommodate every linen order that comes our way, but may clients are wonderful about planning and placing their orders early with only slight revisions before the event. So, the one that refers you and the one that helps you a lot.

EPC: Anything else you want to share about this industry that supports virtually all events?

Carol: Companies have started upgrading their linen inventory so wherever you have party rental people you have more choices and special linens.

I always tell people, "We are a manufacturer. If you buy your own linen fabric, you should buy a sample from us first. This yard of linen, let us wash it for you and make sure you're getting a good fabric that will wash well and allow you to reuse it."

What we discovered a few years ago was we would have some big companies send us linens, and we would wash them, and the color was gone in one or two washes. They were like, "Oh my Gosh, what did you do?" It wasn't that, it was the type of fabric they were purchasing.

So, I think it's more of an education. Don't just buy random fabric because if you pay a little and you think you're getting a lot. You're not going to get a turn on it. You've lost your entire investment. That's an education tool. Always wash it. It's nicer to do a commercial wash. I can wash anything in my home washer, and it works well, but when you put it in a large washer like we have here it can change. It's good to just test things very well before you put it in your inventory, so you have a good turn on them. You can make more money that way with your clients.

EPC: What is the best place for them to go to learn more about you?

Carol: They can go to our website, GBSlinens.com or call 800-700-6448. We ship all over. We started in California in 2004, I put a sales rep in Texas. We now have offices in Houston and San Antonio, and a manufacturing facility in Orlando.

EPC Book Recommendation:

Weddings in Color: 500 Creative Ideas for Designing a Modern Wedding
by Vané Broussard & Minhee Choo

Sometimes when things are falling apart they may be actually falling into place.

CHAPTER 18
Bruce Wawrzyniak
Now Hear This

At the Event Planners Club, we identify what makes experts like Bruce so unique. He captures each client's story and builds a professional brand around it.

EPC: Bruce Wawrzyniak is the owner and president of Tampa, Florida based *Now Hear This*, which specializes in management, promotion and booking in the entertainment industry. Bruce has clients on both coasts and works with singers, songwriters, bands and more. He's been a speaker at the Young Songwriters Workshop that was held at a camp in Nashville, is scheduled to be a panelist at the Driven Music Conference, presented at the Marketing Summit in Tampa and is putting on a Promoting Your Music Career Workshop in Pensacola Beach, Florida. He's also the host of weekly *Now Hear This Entertainment*, with listeners from 120 countries, airing for two-and-a-half years, with guests ranging from participants on *American Idol, The Voice, America's Got Talent,* to Grammy award winners, Rock and Roll Hall of Famers. His show has companionship to the e-book series called *Bruce's Bonus Book, Beginning Tips for Up and Coming Entertainers.*

Bruce: Thanks, I'm excited to share some secrets.

EPC: Let's start with where you grow up?

Bruce: I grew up in the friendly confines of Buffalo, New York. We were a typical family, nose to the ground, going to school, making sure I good grades. My parents instilled the value of hard work. If there was something we wanted, a 10-speed bike or a stereo, then we had to make money so that we can pay for those pleasures ourselves, so that's what I did.

EPC: What did your parents do?

Bruce: My father worked for DuPont and my mother worked for Color Your World, which eventually became Sherwin Williams. My grandfather owned an open-air fruit and vegetable stand at an open-air market. On Saturday mornings I'd join him at his produce stand and that's how I learned about the working world. Sure, I had the typical paper route, but the real learnings were Saturdays with my grandfather. Eventually, became a young entrepreneur with a friend. We started our own lawn mowing business and really thought we had hit it big time when we added a dry cleaner to what had only been residential customers.

EPC: How did you get from produce and lawn care to the music business?

Bruce: I was asked to relocate from Buffalo to New Jersey, but I wanted to relocate to Florida. So, I thought, "Well, if I'm moving out of town, then this is probably about the only time that I'm ever going to relocate." I up and moved to Florida. I started off in Jacksonville for practical reasons as I have an aunt and uncle that live there, so it gave me a place just to get my feet on the ground and start looking for work. When I ended up in the greater Tampa area, I fell in love with the voice of a girl in church choir. Because of my entire background in PR, communications type work, I asked her if there was anything I could do to help her out, if she was singing outside of church. She was and that's how it started.

EPC: How did you get from there?

Bruce: That was something where I was really doing it just because I admired this high school girl's voice. Her dad was a real estate agent and I thought she could really use some help since she didn't know anything about promoting herself. I had success promoting her, even though it started as a side job. Soon I realized, "I can make a business out of this." I was enjoying the role very much as well, and I thought, "This is exactly what I'm going to do. I'm going to go from volunteering to help this girl to actually making a company." *Now Hear This* was formally created in 2004.

EPC: What systems did you put in place to attract clients, other than the first girl you were working with?

Bruce: It became a combination of things. You would start hearing about different events around town. I would go out looking for talent. I would get myself into events that needed judges so that I could find talent myself. I teamed up with a local recording studio and started making contacts that way in terms of referrals, them sending clients to me, me getting tips from them on where some events were around town where I could find and identify talent. Those really laid the foundation for what eventually became quite a referral system.

I was in a part of town, and still am, that isn't the city of Tampa proper, so it's uncharted territory in terms of the towns that are in this area not really having anybody around that's looking for talent like themselves.

EPC: What are some of the biggest mistakes you're finding these performers, entertainment, they're making that you're helping them fix.

Bruce: A lot of them just are so set in their ways that they don't really have the information, quite frankly, about promoting themselves. They're so focused on getting out there and getting more gigs and performing, what they're not realizing is that there's so, so, so much competition that they need to have a story to tell and they need to build their brand through that way. Instead of just saying, "I'm good. This is my price. When can I play there?" they must have a track record, they have to have something that's going to get the attention of the venue that they're trying to get booked at. Otherwise, they're no different than every other email that's coming in, every other phone call that's coming in, every other unsolicited stop-in that a lot of these people are doing to the places they want to play at.

I've really shaped each client's story for them and built a professional image that they can be proud of. From their website to their official YouTube channel to their demo tape, it's got to be a first-class presentation. Performers typically have an attitude of, "I'm good. I've been playing for X amount of time. This is my rate, which is very competitive. Please book me."

EPC: What type of services do you help them with? What does a typical client hire you for, and how does that work?

Bruce: I have a long menu of services and customize so it's not "Do you want Package A, Package B, or Package C." If I'm working with a band, say, of four guys who are all in their 50s that just want to play here in the Tampa Bay area on the weekend, they're going to need an entirely distinct set of services from say, a 19-year-old girl who's a singer/songwriter that wants to do original music for a career, doesn't mind traveling and sees herself wanting to do this full time someday.

I will offer things like, "Let me get you booked somewhere." I will offer things like, "Let me get you some interviews on radio, on TV, in the newspaper, Internet, podcasts." I will offer services like, "If you are doing original music, let me do what a manager should be doing in the music business, which is get your music copyrighted for you, let's get to the studio and get you recording. In the meantime, I'll get a photographer. We'll set up a photo shoot. We'll get a graphic designer to do the artwork for your CD. I'll work on the actual distribution so your music's getting out onto iTunes, Spotify, CD Baby, all that kind of stuff. Then, of course, the actual manufacturing of the CD's as well as, of course, behind the scenes. Doing a website for them. Overseeing their social media for them." There's really an extensive list of services. It's even things like their stage presence. Filming them, not only so that we have video for them online and pictures for the same, but watching them, sitting down with that video and looking and saying, "Here are the good things that you're doing and here are a couple things that you have to work on."

What I love is that they're all so critical of themselves that when I start rolling that video, they watch it and they'll automatically start critiquing themselves, so I don't have to come across as the bad guy. Even though I lead with the positives, they eventually see, "Wow, I really do this a lot." Or, "Wow, I really need to change that." This whole list that I'm giving to you right now is the whole package, the whole professional image that we want to present, because again, the old, "You only have one chance to make a good first impression," over my lengthy career of doing this, I have had lots of examples of, "You never know who's going to be in the audience," good stories that I love to tell. As a result, that means that you really do always have to put your best foot forward, yes on the stage, but on your website, on the materials that you have at your live performances and so on, so that when this one person does come along, they look at you and they say, "I like this person. I want to help them. They're doing things right."

EPC: What sort of systems do you have in place to deliver what they're looking for?

Bruce: Again, a lot of those projects that I talked about, a lot of those services that I offer are very tangible. Those are things that someone can hand over. Here's my merchandise. Here's my CD. Here's my website address, check me out online. I have these tangibles that they can look at and say, "Okay, wow. Bruce has given me a lot of things, and in return, outsiders can look at them and say, 'Wow, I like what this person is doing.'"

The thing that I thought I was doing to market my own business was to launch the podcast that you mentioned in the intro because I thought, I do have to attract new clients to my business, and I thought if I have this podcast, there's going to be someone listening in "insert city here" that's going to say, "This guy sounds like he knows his stuff. I should see if he can manage me." As is the case with so many of the new mediums that come along over the years, as you well know, the world of podcasting is just so huge that it's really turned into an animal in and of itself. That's why when I am servicing my own clients, I will make sure that when I'm looking for interview opportunities for them, it will be the traditional, radio, TV, newspaper, internet, but I'm also making sure to get them on podcasts also because a lot of these guests that I'm talking to each week are telling me how much collaboration they're doing with people that they're finding on the internet, with people that they're finding on Sound Cloud, with people that they're finding on platforms like that.

It's really opened a tremendous opportunity for performers nowadays, for songwriters especially, that they can collaborate with other people online. If I can put my clients into positions of visibility where they can be found, then more doors are going to open for them.

EPC: With all that you've done and all the success you've achieved and the amazing relationships you've got, what's your biggest challenge now?

Bruce: Time management because there's not enough hours in the day. I'm thrilled with the level of clients that I'm starting to get approached by in terms of potential clients, but fitting that all into a day that doesn't go from the morning I wake up until the moment that I go to sleep at night, really becomes a challenge. I'm trying to put some things in place internally to make that more manageable and at the same time, if I see that I'm still giving my clients what they need and what they want and no one's really suffering, no one's really lacking, then at least I can continue to put these new things into place behind the scenes so that it's a seamless transition to only being able to work for them more efficiently.

EPC: What is the best advice? What has been your lowest and your highest entrepreneurial moment and what did you learn from that?

Bruce: I would say my highest entrepreneurial moment would just be on behalf of a client, but I think it's testimony to my work ethic which is one of those opportunities where I had someone out performing and someone just really took to her and came to me and one thing led to another and they said, "I've got some contacts," this is here in Florida, "I've got some contacts back in California where I used to live. I'd love to see your girl here really get some big opportunities open to her," and lo and behold, a couple months later I was sitting in a coffee shop in Hollywood having lunch with someone who, to this day, I have stayed in touch with and have met with as I've continued to go out to California. This is someone, mind you, that's been nominated for an Emmy award, been nominated for two Golden Globes and just has music credits that would impress anybody that read his resume, whether they know much about the music business or not.

That was a real high point for me, to have her in a position where, obviously, the song and the talent must be there, but to be able to turn that meeting, that chance meeting at a performance, into me sitting with someone who I've now nurtured into a very trusted contact, very respected contact, really has been a highlight for me.

In terms of a low point, anytime you lose a client, it's a low point and you need to learn something from it. One person stands out in that this was one of those young girl stories where I saw the potential and she didn't have anyone working for her. We got started and I didn't sign her to an agreement right away. I just got to work and started doing for her what I do for everyone else and had my agreement with the attorney, asking like, "I think it's time that we redo this from now on for people that sign with me." This girl fell into that gray area and I was two-and-a-half months in with nothing signed and she disappeared and didn't pay me a penny for all the work that I'd put in.

What I learned then is get everybody to sign even before you do the first hour of work for them. Hopefully, 95 percent of the time the people will be honest and will have no intention of walking away from you like this case. I realized that being a nice guy and going into business, you can't be so nice that you just trust everybody thinking "Of course, they're going to pay me." Everyone since then has signed with Now Hear This before I've started working for them.

EPC: With all that is constantly changing in your world, how do you stay on top of it all?

Bruce: I'm glad that you asked that because my blog that I'm writing today is about professional development and encouraging young performers that you can't just focus on, "How is my stage show, how is my songwriting, how is my album coming along." They need to get out and network. They need to do professional development and so what I do is I keep my hand in all these different things. I belong to a chamber of commerce. I belong to a business owners' group. I belong to a podcasters association. I do read industry blogs. These diverse types of events that I attend, whether it's a social media marketing world, whether it's podcast movement, whether it's a Google summit, a Facebook summit, these things all keep me current, as best as I can, on all the different things that I need to know about that I can in turn, apply towards servicing my clients every day.

EPC: For those clients, who is an ideal client for you?

Bruce: There are really two sides to that question in that the clients that are paying me on a regular basis, on a monthly retainer, they are performers. At the same time, I do have some non-music clients. I have an Olympic athlete. I have some authors. I have a couple small businesses.

The flip side of that is clients in the sense that if I'm booking someone to perform somewhere, I'm considering that venue to be my client that night, even though we may not have a long-lasting ongoing agreement where I'm sending them entertainment continually, I do want them to have an enjoyable experience with me so that they'll say, "That person that Bruce sent us was really great. The next time we need entertainment, we're going to contact Now Hear This again." Those are the ones that I've been spending more time on lately, is trying to find those clients and make sure that I do have more and more venues and events for my performers to go and perform at.

That could be restaurants, that could be weddings, that could be corporate events, that could be you name it. Anyplace that is looking for live entertainment, I want to be in the conversation so that they know that they can call *Now Hear This* and the variety of options to choose from.

EPC: Where can event planners go to learn more about you?

Bruce: Www.nowhearthis.biz

EPC Book Recommendation:

What They'll Never Tell You About the Music Business, Third Edition: The Complete Guide for Musicians, Songwriters, Producers, Managers, Industry Executives, Attorneys, Investors, and Accountants by Peter M. Thall

CHAPTER 19
Adam Wilber
Inventor/Speaker/Magician

At the Event Planners Club, we identify what makes experts like Adam so unique. He books creativity time. This led to his inventing PYRO, the fireball shooter.

EPC: Adam Wilber, is a leading magician, for corporate entertainment. He travels across the US and Canada performing, lecturing and speaking on creativity, design, and imagination. He has been in Sci-Fi and on CNET, NBC, ABC and FHM. Adam has performed for Trump, Hilton, Trump hotel collection, IBM, and Wizard Wars. Literally any media outlet you can imagine. I think he has a total of a million and a half YouTube views. He is a celebrity magician, an amazing entertainer, somebody who blows my mind any time I see him work.

Adam: Thanks, it's a real pleasure.

EPC: How'd you get started in magic?

Adam: I started when I was six. A buddy of mine showed me a trick at his house while we were hanging out, and it blew my mind. I said, "Show me how it's done." He refused. I found the book at the library, learned the trick, and then went home and showed my father. At six years old, my dad is a very engineer-minded guy, and I saw the look of true astonishment in his face and it turned my life around. When I fooled my father, and he said, "How did you do it," I was hooked. I've been studying magic for the last 30 years. Every bit of magic whether it's creating, performing, lecturing, or teaching.

EPC: You have performed for some of the biggest names all over the world. While a lot of people pick up a magic set or magic book, you made a career out of it, and became an international celebrity. How did you do that?

Adam: My claim to fame in the magic world was about six years ago. I'd been working and performing, but also working jobs. I was never performing to the standard where I could support a family and children, which I now have achieved. I decided I wanted to get known in the magic community, so I approached a company, and said, "Look, I'm available. If you need anything, let me know." I got a foot in the door of the company called illusionists.com, as their forum director, doing a couple hours a week looking over their forums.

I bulldogged my way in. I kept putting out ideas and different presentations that I thought would work for the company and worked my way into a full-time job at the company. Once I got that, I created a device called Pyro. Pyro's a fireball shooter you can strap onto your wrist, show your hand's empty, and shoot fireballs. I developed that over the course of two years. When we launched, my goal was to launch it to the magic community, but I knew that tech and gadget people would also be drawn to this device. Through our marketing and some creative viral videos, the thing went nuts, and it went viral. It got me on so many different new agencies. When people hear fireball shooter, it turns people's heads. That was my big claim to fame. I was on interviews with Discovery, and I got it featured on all these different magazines, Maximum and CNN, CBS, and NBC.

That was the real, "Who is this guy," which was when I launched this device Pyro. A lot of the performing stemmed from that. I got interviews where they wanted to interview me about Pyro, I was more focused on the fact that I'm available to entertain at your event. That snowballed my success to where I am today. It also brought me up to the rankings of general manager and overseeing the entire company of illusionists. Illusionist is the largest online magic company in the world. It's been around the longest. It's one of the most prestigious and well known. Now I get to run that company, and that helped build my clout in the magic community. That really helped my performing and getting recognized across the country.

Next month, I'll be in the UK lecturing to magicians and teaching them my magic. It really all stems from developing that one viral product, Pyro.

EPC: That is incredible, and you're not a one hit wonder. You've invented some of the highest selling magic effect in the world, and you lecture on creativity. How do you get your ideas? Where do you find your inspiration from?

Adam: My inspiration comes from all over the place. The last couple of years, a lot of the inspiration I get is from my children, and watching them. I think with creativity, a lot of people have this idea that creativity is a God given gift that you're born with it, or you're not. To some people that is true, but that's a very small percentage of people. Just like some people are musically talented that they're born and at four years old, they can play Beethoven. Most people study, practice, and set the time aside to become better. Creativity's no different.

The way I get most of my ideas is forcing myself to sit down and be creative. I think that's what most people forget to do. They fear creativity and while maybe they hit a road block and say, "I'm not creative." That's just not the case. It's just about being persistent, having a goal in mind and then focusing. I stress the word focusing time for creativity, uninterrupted time every single day. Just like a world class athlete, every single day, regardless of how they feel, they make time to work out and better their craft. It's the same with creativity.

A lot of my inspiration comes from knowing the magic industry very well, and I know what products will sell, and I know what products will help other entertainers be memorable. I focus on creating magic that fits into that. I want it to be very memorable for the audience, and I also want it to be sellable. I want it to be something magicians will see and say I want to have that.

A lot of the creating I do is to sit down and say what's going to sell well, and what's going to help entertainers be a more memorable performer? Then it's just dedicated, focused time in sitting down and becoming creative.

EPC: Scheduling time each day to force yourself to be creative, that's a secret. People think that inspiration just hits like a lightning bolt or it just shows up.

Adam: I think the biggest and most important thing is realizing everybody is creative in one aspect or another. It's knowing that you are creative and having a goal. If your goal is, "I want to sell magic," great. That's what I'm going to sit down and create. If your goal is, "I want to develop a speech help people be more innovative," then that's where your creative flowing needs to come from. It's knowing what your end goal is and then sitting down every single day. I have an allotted time every day that don't let life interrupt me. I have my morning routine, and right after my morning routine is my creativity session. Regardless of how I feel that day, I'm sitting down, and I am forcing myself to be uninterrupted and to create.

Now with that said, half the time nothing comes of it. It can be frustrating, but at the end of the day, the half the time that nothing's coming from it, that's when a lot of the creativity is happening. You might be sitting there not getting ideas, but you're building up a bank of ideas that at some point will hit you like a lightning bolt. Some people do see something in a passing and get a great idea from it. It's allowing yourself to be open to accept those things.

I saw my kid do something the other day, and I went, "Wow, that was interesting, what can I do with that?" The next day, I started thinking about it during my creativity session, and now I'm working on developing a beautiful stage presentation for a standup trick based on what I saw my kid do. I'm opening my mind to absorbing and being ready to take in anything as a creative outlet. It's him playing with some building blocks, and I went, "Everybody can relate to that, that's cool, there's something there. "

EPC: You have performed at so many events and places. What are the biggest mistakes you run across when it comes to people planning a corporate event?

Adam: First, it was not hiring a professional. The biggest mistake somebody can do is price shop on entertainment. People must fit into budgets, and I understand that, but when you start looking for an entertainer and say, "I'm going to price out three or four more," and you hire somebody based solely on their price, you're getting what you pay for. The problem there is that to be a real professional entertainer is a lot different than being somebody that can do some tricks. Anybody that can do some tricks today can develop a website and some marketing material that makes them look like a true professional. When you're booking an entertainer, the biggest mistake I see is not doing your diligence to find out if that entertainer is going to fit exactly the needs you have.

Some people are great at making people laugh, while other people are great at giving a message and tweaking your message into an entertaining way as opposed to getting up there and doing tricks to make people laugh. It's knowing what your goal is for the event. If it's just entertainment, then finding somebody who specializes in that and then doing your diligence to make sure this person can walk the walk. Ask for some references. Ask to say, "Do you have a few clients that fit into my group?" I work at a company that has 100 employees, and we're a tech company, have you ever worked with somebody in that field, and if so, do you have a number I could call to just talk to them?

Then the second thing is not really listening to the expert. I've had people say, "We want you for 200 people, and it's going to be a 30-minute show, but you're going to be in the middle of the room surrounded." I tell them no. I absolutely can't perform that way because it's not going to work. Well that's the way the venue is so we must do it that way. What they don't realize is they're paying top dollar. They need to listen to the professional to make sure they're getting the best benefit of their money. If you put a magician or an entertainer in a room and surround them 360 degrees, you're not going to get the best show. Half the people will see a magic show. The other half of the people will see the back of the magician's suit.

My job as the performer is to find out what the needs are and work to my best to make sure we can give them more than they're bargaining for. Whereas I know if somebody says you're going to be performing surrounded that my show what they're asking for is not going to work. I need to politely say then I'm not the performer for you. Where a lot of performers will just say, "I'll do it."

Listening to the performer is an important thing and making sure that what they specialize in will work for

211

what the needs for what your event are.

EPC: What are some of your event secrets that an event planner could use to make their event unforgettable?

Adam: I think it depends on what the event is. If you're looking for pure entertainment, then there's tons of different things. The thing to keep in mind is, in Marketing 101, nobody cares about anything but themselves. That's the reality of the way we are put together as human beings. It is imperative for our survival to care first and foremost about ourselves. That sounds very selfish, but it's the reality. If you want to put an event together that people are going to remember, then it can't be focused around one person, or one speaker, one cool DJ, or a photo booth. It needs to be focused around what do my attendees want, and what are they going to take home because it directly relates to them or it directly impacts them?

You want to build the event around what's going to benefit in one way or another your attendees. Not what's going to look the best for one person or maybe the VIP or the boss. Of course, you need to please your boss, but if you're putting an event together for multiple people to have an enjoyable time, then you need to focus on what's going to be fun for those individuals. A lot of times an entertainer is just that. A DJ may play music that half of the audience likes, but the other half doesn't. A good entertainer can really relate to everybody in the audience, regardless if it's the CEO or if it's somebody that just does landscaping for the company. That's what I think good entertainment should be is relating to everybody in the audience.

With that said, you're not going to connect with everybody, but the goal at any event should be connecting and making a lasting connection with people. Whether that's a kick-off meeting to start your first quarter of the year and getting people pumped up and excited about the year to come. You need to connect to them in a way they care about that means something to them as opposed to coming out and saying, "Let's really do an excellent job this year, let's hit these numbers, and here's why we need to." More, let's all look individually at what we can do to better ourselves first and in turn, we will better our sales and our bottom line.

I think the main thing is focusing on the individuals and making connections with them as opposed to an overall event, what are we going to do to make this event great? If you focus on the attendees and what's really going to resonate with them personally, then you're setting yourself up for success, whether that's with your entertainment, with your food choices, with your venue. It just needs to be focused on connecting with them individually because that's what people care about. They care about themselves.

EPC: What's the best advice you've ever gotten?

Adam: There's different advice for everything; as far as performance, as far as marketing. I would say the best nugget of advice I've ever received is something in the lines of that. If you want to be a professional who makes living doing performance art, then you need to realize it's not about you. Getting on stage, it should never be about you. If you're trying to be a performer, which a lot of performers are because they want to be popular, and they want to be recognized, and they want people to say that guy was amazing. You might get some work, and you could probably be pretty good if you put the time into it, but you're not going to make an impact on people. To make an impact on people, it's got to be about sharing an emotional experience with them. I think too many performers focus on the tricks and fooling people or looking good on stage as opposed to emotionally connecting with an audience and giving them something, giving them a gift of entertainment.

Entertainment is the lack of boredom. If you put me in front of a group of 200 people, my job is to know what these people are about and then entertain them so for that 45 minutes or 30 minutes. They're not thinking about their taxes that are due, or their oil that needs to be changed, or the big deadline that they're facing. They're thinking about life and enjoying life for that short amount of time just having fun and being entertained. I think that thing to really know at least as a performer and the piece of advice that I really sit well with is it's not about me on stage.

It's about what I can give to the audience. I want them to have an emotional ride of fun, laughs, and a bit of wonder, and to realize this world is full of magic everywhere you look. It's like Ferris Bueller said, "You've got to slow down and look." I think that was one of the biggest pieces that stuck with me was to not think that it's about me but realize that I'm up there to perform for an audience and they should be the focus of what my presentations are about.

EPC: Is it important to know your ideal client?

Adam: Yes, my ideal client is an adult audience, 22 years old and older, which could be a corporation that wants to get some messages across. I do some trade show work where I'll work with clients that want to build leads. They want the leads that are walking by their booth to stop, notice them, and listen to their message. That's a perfect client for me is a corporation that's got a message that they want to put across in a fun and entertaining way, something a little different, as well as any group of people that wants to be entertained in a clean, comedic, light hearted way. Those are the groups that I work best with.

EPC: Where should event planners go to see your amazing testimonials and how you've got people talking about how unforgettable you are, how everybody was standing up and cheering, whistling and screaming, and raving about your show?

Adam: Here's my contact information: info@adamwilber.com and www.magicadam.com

---

EPC Book Recommendation:

Creativity, Inc.: Overcoming The Unseen Forces That Stand in the Way of True Inspiration
by Ed Catmull & Amy Wallace

HAPPINESS
is contagious,
pass it on.

CHAPTER 20
Hank Yuloff
Sedona Marketing Retreats

At the Event Planners Club, we identify what makes experts like Hank so unique. His cutting-edge business insights make for a colorful life outlook that matches his Sedona Mountain backdrop.

EPC: Hank Yuloff is a targeted marketing tactician with 30 years' experience keeping companies on the top of mind with their customers. He began his career working for various media outlets before opening his own company in 1997, which was recently re-branded as SedonaMarketing.com.

Hank: Living in Sedona is fantastic, I look outside our windows and all I see is red rocks and forests.

EPC: Did you grow up in Arizona?

Hank: I grew up in Los Angeles. I am a product of the LA Unified school district, then attended San Diego State. Then I went back to Los Angeles to start my career.

EPC: What was your childhood like?

Hank: My dad was a pharmacist, which meant my summer jobs were spent being a delivery boy for various independent pharmacies because he knew the owners and got me the jobs. My parents were married for over 50 years before my mom passed away. You hear these stories of people who overcame great struggle in their life. I had a wonderful childhood and upbringing.

EPC: Okay. What did you do after you graduated San Diego State?

Hank: My first job was for a direct mail company and I worked for them for 3.5 years. Then, I worked for a promotional products company for a long time. As a sales manager, I excelled and was on the president's club team as a top earner. My career took a turn when the company owner hired his son, who knew nothing about the industry, to be the sales manager.

I decided to open up my own promotional products company, which turned into clients asking for help on trade shows? Hey, can you help me with some other marketing things going on? We refocused the company and now about half of what we do are marketing plans and that's increasing to almost all marketing programs.

EPC: What inspired you to write the books?

Hank: The first one, the 49 Stupid with the business cards, as marketing people, we always tell your clients, one of the best tools you can use to market you, is to have a book. You're not going to get rich on it but it's a great awesome tool to market you. Other people hand a brochure, you can hand them a book that shows them you're the expert.

I see so many business cards. Last night I was at a

chamber event and got 3 or 4 cards that didn't have websites, I can help people with that. My business coach looked at me and said that's a terrific book, but you've told people their cards suck, why don't you do a workbook to help them create better cards. I started that and 160 something pages later turned into the marketing checklist.

I still haven't done a workbook for the first book, but The Marketing Checklist, 80 Simple Ways to Master your Marketing. The new one which is going to come out on Amazon in July of this year, is the Marketing Checklist to 49 More Simple Ways.

What I do is we're always looking for ways for companies to help market themselves and we save them and put them in the book.

EPC: That is awesome. You've had such an incredible journey and such a cool transition. What do you wish you knew when you got started?

Hank: Such a good question. Here's what happens with most companies or most business owners and entrepreneurs. We are taught to do what we do, or we get expertise in it. Whether it's planning meetings, we find out we have a knack for this and you develop that skill. I was doing a coaching call with a client today that's a lawyer. He went to law school and was taught the law. No one is really taught either in school or professionally how to market what they do.

What I wish I had learned originally is the idea you need to put a team together, a talented team, a financial person, a banker, legal people. You need to have all of those when you're starting. It so often seems people say I'll get that afterwards, I just need to get the doors open. You need those folks that you can rely on and fall back on. I wish I had that at the beginning.

For us, I was in Thanksgiving of '96 we went around the table and my mom said, "You seem happy in your personal life but what's going on in work?" I said, "I'm not really happy." I explained the situation. She said, "What would it take to start your own business?" I said, "I have clients, I know where to get all these promotional products. My professional stuff. I really just need a fax machine." I was going to have to return my fax machine to the company that owned it. She looked at my dad and she said, "Write him a check."

EPC: That's a nice mom.

Hank: Yeah. My mom was the entrepreneur in our family. She always had something going on. She sold handbags and jewelry. She always had some retail stuff going on. She's the one that sparked that. I didn't really think of I need to have an incredible accountant for business. I need to establish relationship with banks and all those things that you need when you're becoming successful and I think it makes sense that you have it when you start I think that's very important.

EPC: I think that is absolutely true. Let's play a little bit here. What are some of the most common mistakes someone like that would be making with their business cards and their marketing and how can you help them?

Hank: Let's start with the business cards first. I am a strong believer; you need to have all the contact information there. Remember, your business card is designed for people to get an impression, but they need to be able to track you down. Most of the time, it's so they can go to your website and check you out. We'll get to your website in a second.

Your card must have easy contact info. I also think you need to have an address on there because even if you're using one of those PO box types places, because it shows you're professional. People like to know where you are. That's the argument I get most when it comes to cards. Honestly if somebody's listening and you send me an email with your card I'll give you a free evaluation of it and give you some tips. Make it simple, make it easy, easy to read, logo, all the basics and while still not trying to make it do too much.

The next thing, people are going to check you out before they hire you. This is a hugely important day. One of the seminal moments in their life. Your website needs to represent exactly what you're doing. The challenge I've seen, I've looked at a lot of wedding industry websites, and they're very cookie cutter. It's the same kind of stuff. They'll use stock photos of weddings they didn't do. Wait a minute. Why are you doing that?

You need to either get on good terms with the photographers who are doing the events you're planning and get some incredible photos, not juts he photos the bride and groom want but the photos that show you in action, your team in action.

EPC: That's a good tip.

Hank: You should get video of that too. They're shooting video of the bride and groom but get video of your team working, making sure everything works. All the little stuff that goes into it. That becomes your sizzle real because people will be watching that. They're going to say, "They get it. They're not just showing me pictures of other people's weddings." This is important.

Find an excellent web designer and be willing to pay the money for good stuff. It's important that you're doing that. Make sure you're blogging on your website and if your website is built in WordPress, you'll have a much easier time of it. I don't like any of the cookie cutter sites. There's I won't mention the names of those. You can get your website for free because the search engine optimization on those is not going to help you, it's going to help them. Remember, if the product is free that you're using, you are the product. On Facebook, it's free because we are the product. That's why those ads are there on the right side. If it's built in WordPress, you should be blogging. I'm not asking for War and Peace in your blog. I'm looking for 300 to 500 words most of the time, which we all learn to do in high school. There's 3 points you must make about the book and the final one is the conclusion. You can use this approach for a blog. If you do it with a video it makes your sales process much simpler when you sit down with them in person.

EPC: Absolutely. How can an event planner differentiate themselves when there are dozens and dozens of folks who say, "I can do your wedding" in their town or in their city?

Hank: This is going to be a hard one. I think the more that you can socialize in what you are doing, the more you can niche it down. Let me give you some examples. Your wonderful LGBT community or specialize in people that are over 50 that have found love again. Or people with their second weddings, people with kids, or 20-somethings. If there's a niche that you relate to incredibly, then you'll know what they're thinking before they ask it, the better off you will be.

In our industry, there are tons of people who can do marketing plans for companies. Dozens and dozens. My wife and I have a specific specialty. We work well with couple owned businesses. We also work well with business owners that are 50 and older that are nowhere near retiring, but they feel that technology is passing them by. We have different programs that we set up for our different niches.

There are certain industries we don't touch. It might make you cringe to turn down that wedding, but if you're just going to compete with others, why waste your time putting the proposal together if it's not something that you specialize in?

EPC: That makes a lot of sense. What is the best advice you've ever received?

Hank: Always tell the truth to your clients no matter how much it hurts. On the promotional products side of our business, we've always had a policy if a product came in wrong, it's our fault not theirs. Even if they approved the proof, hey look, we're going to make it right. I tell them you did approve the proof but we're going to make it right and we're going to make it happen. On the marketing side, we've had clients where we've had a conversation last night with somebody, they want to re-brand their company.

I had to give them some very honest news about the name you're choosing is not going to work for you. It's going to hurt you, in fact. We had to have that very heart to heart talk and I know I'm doing them a service in the long run. I think that's always been the best advice. It's "Take a breath, tell them the truth, move forward."

EPC: That is great advice. What would you do differently if you had to start over?

Hank: I would have come to Sedona a lot earlier. We only got to Sedona last year and part of it was my dad had dementia and we were the ones taking care of him. The last year or so of his life we couldn't move him. I think that when we made the decision that assisted living was it, I think if we had brought him to the Arizona area earlier, we still would have been able to see him every day and it would have saved us a couple of years, and I think he really would have liked it here.

Other than that, I don't know. I feel we're all on a path and we get where we're supposed to go when we're supposed to get there. I think I can look at that change and it's one we had a definite plan that eventually we would get here, we would come to Sedona, we would open the retreat center, we would do this, but I think I might have included that earlier.

EPC: Awesome. Who's an ideal client for you?

Hank: Let me introduce you to Harriet. When somebody listening to this, whatever picture of Harriet you have in your mind, hold on to that for a second and now let me explain who Harriet is. Harriet is 45 to 60 years old. She is the right-hand man of the guy or girl that owns the company. I have met Harriet 8 separate times in my career running an orthodontist office, rental yard, a small chain of banks. I've met her in various places. In fact, a chain of schools.

Self designates Christian. Vacation life is built around her vacation with grandchildren. Anyone that in the company that runs afoul of Harriet will not be with the company very long because the guy or girl that runs the company knows that she is the one that's really running the company. Most people when they meet Harriet they just think that she is the gatekeeper as opposed to she is making the HR decisions, she's making the marketing decisions, she's making a whole lot of decisions for that company because the one that's running it is too busy in the sales mode to deal with the other stuff.

That's one of my favorite avatars. Any time we're marketing, if you can have two or three of your prime avatars, that helps you when you meet them. I mentioned earlier, my wife and I like married couples and this avatar is early 30's to mid-40's. They've started a business, they've had some success. All our clients that use us usually they've gotten to a certain level and they know there's more. They want to grow to the next level. They need some help with getting their messaging down. We know that the challenges of couple run businesses, because my wife and I have been doing it, we're not relationship coaches, but how are they going to split activities in the business, how are they going to message, how are they going to market them as the product as opposed to let's say we're wedding planners as opposed to my wife and I are the planners. We're the ones that do it. The generic. We love couple owned businesses. Those are incredible for us.

EPC: What is the first step you would want them to take?

Hank: When you are looking at marketing your business, begin with the end in mind. Let me explain. Take an ad here or promote your podcast there. It's basically they're selling a marketing tactic of some sort.

When somebody's approaching you to put an ad here or do this or that, begin with the end in mind. What is your marketing goal? Who's that target market, and is that tactic, is that going to help you? If you think yeah, it's going to help me, what's the message and what's the consistent message that I need to use when I do that so that it's going to work?

When we do marketing plans for companies one of the first things we do is look at all the shiny objects. We all have them. We've all done some marketing thing that we thought was going to be awesome and it's a bright shiny object that some sales person that just wants to make a commission held in front of us and we've done it. You should begin with the end in mind. Know the message you want to give out and if that marketing tactic doesn't work out, no matter how attractive it is, don't do it. Use the tactics that are going to work for you the most.

EPC: What is the first place you would want people to go to learn more about you?

Hank: We have a blog, Sedonamarketingretreats.com. In fact, you can just go to Sedonamarketing.com and it will refer you over. Read our blog. We have so much free information on there. Help your marketing. You may decide you want to work with us, and that's cool, would love to have you as a client, but get educated. We live in a Google world. You can find out how to do tons of different things.

If you go there, use our free information. Let us help you out even if you don't know who we are. If I could do one more thing, one more marketing thing that you guys need to do, video is your friend. Facebook has said that in the next few years, most posts are going to be video. You need to get used to how you react on video and work on video and use video to promote you. Put that, turn that to your advantage. Start getting comfortable being in front of the camera and sharing your message that way.

EPC Book Recommendation:

Hank's Books: *49 Stupid Things People Do With Business Cards and How to Fix Them*, and *The Marketing Checklist, 80 Simple Ways to Master Your Marketing.*

CONCLUSION

Back at the very beginning of this book, we talked about time well spent. We certainly hope you agree that the time you spent reading this book fits that category.

And we hope you got as much out of reading these interviews as we did conducting them. We're so grateful to these creative, innovative, and successful people for sharing their experience, and expertise.

We hope you'll use the insights and information in the way they intended: to make your events more memorable, make your business more successful, and make your lives easier. That's why we did this book.

That's also our goal at the Event Planners Club. Our members are always sharing with each other and learning from each other. From best practices to case studies, from things that worked especially well to things that just plain flopped.

If you're trying to grow your event planning business, we hope you'll consider joining our community. If you'd like to learn more about who we are and what we do, go to https://eventplannersclub.com/ or give us a call at 510-594-0828.

As an event planner, there's nothing like that feeling you get when you've created a memorable event. Don't you want to have that feeling every time?

Made in the USA
Las Vegas, NV
30 November 2021

35669783R10136